Bond Vigilantes

Fifth anniversary book

GW00545578

Authors

1. Jim Leaviss
2. Mike Riddell
3. Richard Woolnough
4. Anthony Doyle
5. Stefan Isaacs
6. Ben Lord
7. Matthew Russell
8. Tamara Burnell
9. Gordon Harding
10. Markus Peters
11. Stuart Liddle
12. Filippo Fabbris
13. James Tomlins
14. James Thompson
15. Jeff Spencer
16. Vladimir Jovkovic

Published by M&G Investment Management Limited

Copyright © M&G Investment Management Limited 2012

ISBN 978-0-9571340-0-3

Printed and bound in Great Britain by Pureprint Group Limited (incorporating Beacon Press)

Introduction

When we chose the name Bond Vigilantes for our blog in 2006, we thought the term was purely an historical curiosity. The Bond Vigilantes had had two great periods of power and influence in the previous three decades. They first came to prominence as institutional fixed interest investors threatened governments with "buyers' strikes" at the end of the 1970s having seen both their capital and income almost wiped out by persistent double digit inflation in the western economies. This led to the appointment of Paul Volker as the Chairman of the US Federal Reserve in 1979, and the setting of interest rates above the rate of inflation, rather than below it. Inflation peaked at nearly 15% in 1980, and fell year after year from then on in – and bonds became an investible asset class again. The second period of influence came during the Clinton presidency, when the bond markets made it clear that yields would rise on any hint that budget deficits were going to rise. As Clinton's advisor James Carville said at the time, "I used to think that if there was reincarnation, I wanted to come back as the president or the pope or a .400 baseball hitter. But now I want to come back as the bond market. You can intimidate everybody".

By 2006 then, bond markets had nothing to worry about, and the Bond Vigilantes name had fallen out of use. After all, inflation was dead, thanks to a combination of globalisation, the internet, demographics, and those independent central bankers who believed they had won the war against the persistent price rises of the `70s and early `80s. Budget deficits were also something that didn't need worrying about. Above trend economic growth (and in many cases some accounting tricks that hid government debt away from the balance sheet) meant that government bond issuance was low and stable. Bonds really were "risk free" – and not just in the world of the AAA government bond markets. In 2006, credit spreads were hitting record lows, and default risk was regarded as so negligible that an entire industry sprung up to lever up those riskless credit investments.

As we started our blog then, we had a front row seat at the beginnings of the Great Financial Crisis. We wrote about that new industry, as structured credit products like CDOs and CLOs took off, about the rise of consumer indebtedness, and as far back as 2006 we noted a small article in a US newspaper about a sharp rise in mortgage delinquencies in a suburb of Chicago (perhaps the

Ground Zero of the credit crisis). Of course we didn't get everything right – our bad calls remain on the website for posterity as well as the good ones. In particular a gushing blog in praise of Gordon Brown by one fund manager is gleefully quoted by the rest of us at any opportunity. But on the big calls, I'm very proud of both the accuracy and conviction of our views, and most importantly that those views helped us to outperform for our clients.

We saw that banks were desperately undercapitalised for the losses they would surely face – and that they were also facing liquidity issues owing to their reliance on short term funding. We also realised that the banking sector had become "too big to fail", so their losses would be socialised, putting great strain on sovereign credit ratings and sowing the seeds of the next phase of the crisis.

So with government bonds no longer regarded as risk free, and with inflation high and sticky despite high levels of spare capacity in the global economy, the term Bond Vigilantes passed back into common parlance. I worry sometimes that people might think that we regard ourselves as vigilantes – evil, heartless bastards throwing Greek grandmothers on to the streets, and cackling manically as we try to bring the French government to its knees. It doesn't feel like that from where we sit, running £20 billion of fixed interest in mutual funds for our investors, and you might be surprised to hear that we don't all think that austerity is a great idea, or believe that getting unemployment down is less important than fighting inflation. But it's obviously right that if we think Greek debt is wrongly priced, we mustn't own it. I do however sometimes think of the sketch from "That Mitchell and Webb Look" where a German SS officer turns to another, and pointing to the skull and crossbones insignia on his cap asks "Hans, are we the baddies"? Anyway, we will be more than happy if the Bond Vigilantes name passes back into history, although that's probably some years off.

This book brings together a hundred of our blog posts from the first five years of the website, picked to give a flavour of the developing financial, and then sovereign crises. We have over 12,000 readers each month now, and we very much appreciate the robust debates and challenges we've had from you over the years. We've produced this book in part because it's likely to be our only chance of seeing our words in print (unless my Great British novel starts writing itself), but also because we are using the opportunity to hopefully raise some money for Cancer Research UK, a charity that's close to the hearts of everybody on our team. All proceeds from the book will go directly to them, and if you'd like to donate you can do so at http://www.bondvigilantes.com/anniversary. So finally, thank you for following our blogs and supporting our funds over the years. Thank you to M&G for both taking the leap of faith in allowing us to start blogging in the first place, and also for covering the costs of publication, so that all of the proceeds can go to Cancer Research UK. And thank you to all of the economists, strategists, analysts, friends and family, for ideas and support. A list of acknowledgements can be found at the back of the book.

Jim Leaviss

Contents

2006

2007

2008

2009

2010

2011

o o o o o

2006

Chapter 1
Rates up, unemployment up – inflation up?

Jim Leaviss - Friday, November 10th, 2006

The Bank of England yesterday raised rates to 5%, as expected. With headline inflation at 3.6%, the highest since the middle of 1998, and house prices apparently reaccelerating, this shouldn't have been a surprise to anybody. What's more uncertain is knowing when, and at what level rates will peak.

At the moment I'm not actually too worried about inflation; the reason we're at the currently elevated level is due to a number of "exogenous" shocks, most obviously in energy prices, but also to other non-discretionary items such as a doubling in university tuition fees. It would be worrying though if the UK consumer started to think that this temporary spike up in inflation was more permanent, and started to demand higher wages as a result. Average earnings growth is running at a 4.2% rate, within the Bank of England's tolerance – but the wage setting round is about to begin, and if unions and employees base their demands on the sentiment that inflation is high and persistent, and achieve higher salaries as a result, there's a risk that we get a self-fulfilling prophecy of embedded higher inflation. The Bank has been keen to emphasise that it is expectations of inflation that are the key driver of actual inflation – these exogenous shocks are much less important. And how can they keep inflation expectations down? By hiking rates until we get the message. That's why yesterday's rate hike almost certainly isn't the last in the cycle – another 0.25% in February is likely. On the average mortgage of £90,177 that takes the monthly payment up to £540.38, £26 higher than it was last month. With unemployment rising simultaneously, the wind is gradually being taken out of the sails of the UK consumer.

Chapter 2
Letter from Chicago

Jim Leaviss - Monday, November 20th, 2006

I was in Chicago on business on Friday. Up at 5am with jetlag I was able to take my time reading the Chicago Sun-Times. Two articles in there caught my eye.

First was news of the death of Chicago's own Milton Friedman. Friedman was the ultimate free market economist, arguing for an individual's freedom to buy heroin, and against the necessity of having licensed doctors (the market would determine which were good doctors or not, and at a lower cost than a regulated medical system!). His economic thinking became prevalent during the Reagan and Thatcher years of the 1980s – and his monetarist views informed the importance of targeting of the money supply during this period as a way of fighting inflation. The second article that interested me was a half page feature on the Chicago property market, where there is a definite weakening in demand. Unsold houses are increasingly going to auction. Two houses in the West Pratt area had been up for sale for over a year, and eventually sold at auction in the low $600,000s, having been on the market for $899,000. More weak official housing numbers from the US on Friday reinforced the fact that there appears to be a significant slump taking place over there. Have US rates peaked at 5.25%?

Chapter 3
Home Depot – the first LBO to break $100bn?

Richard Woolnough - Monday, December 4th, 2006

There are rumours in the market that private equity firms are considering bidding for US DIY giant Home Depot. Home Depot's market capitalisation is currently $78bn, so any private equity bidders would have to pay somewhere in the region of $100bn to take over the company. To put this figure in perspective, only six companies in the FTSE 100 have a market cap of over $100bn.

A leveraged buyout (LBO) of this magnitude would send shock waves around the world. Before this year, the $25bn takeover of RJR Nabisco in 1988 was the largest the LBO the world had ever seen. But in July this year, HCA (a US health care company) was LBOd for $33bn, and last month Equity Office (owner of Worldwide Plaza in New York) was bought for $36bn. The market believes that an LBO of $100bn is unlikely, as shown by the fact that the Home Depot's share price has hardly moved, but the fact that there is speculation that such a large takeover could occur is proof that an LBO of this size is potentially on the horizon.

If it does occur, then corporate bond holders better watch out. A leveraged buyout results in a large amount of debt placed on the victim's balance sheet, and inevitably results in multiple credit rating downgrades. LBO targets have traditionally been BBB rated companies as they tend to be smaller companies than their higher rated contemporaries, and are therefore within range of private equity companies. A deal of $100bn would suddenly bring a significant part of the UK corporate bond market into play. Spreads may well then widen out across the board, because LBOs mean higher leverage, which in turn means greater default risk.

Chapter 4
UK inflation surprises to the upside – now watch wages

Jim Leaviss - Tuesday, December 12th, 2006

This morning's inflation data was higher than expected, with the CPI measure targeted by the Monetary Policy Committee coming in at +2.7% from a year ago against +2.4% the previous month. The headline RPI measure was also very strong at +3.9%. For me, the biggest risk to further UK rate hikes remains the prospect of workers seeing this headline rate of inflation approaching 4% (it's not been there since mid 1998) and demanding higher wages in the forthcoming pay bargaining rounds. For all the MPC's focus on the CPI, the public still look to the RPI as their preferred measure – and why not? After all given that housing is a huge factor in our spending why should it be excluded from the inflation data as it is in the CPI? Income Data Services, a consultancy, have pointed out that Ford, Rolls Royce and the Air Traffic Controllers – amongst others – all have automatic pay links to the RPI rather than the CPI.

Looking at the breakdown of the inflation numbers, it's clear that a major factor has been the growth in household bills, and especially energy costs. They are up 11.1% year on year – the highest increase ever recorded. This again is a worry, not least for those on low incomes such as the elderly where this non-discretionary spending forms a much larger percentage of their "personal" inflation basket than for the average where falls in the prices of plasma screen TVs, CDs, and designer clothes can offset part of the rise in fuel bills. Even for those of us who do benefit from deflation in these other items, the regular increases in utility bills have been much more memorable, and newsworthy.

So far wage inflation has remained very well behaved. In the third quarter of this year it was running at a +3.9% rate (i.e. at the same rate as current headline inflation) – so in fact the workforce has not been able to increase its "real" take home pay, despite a small increase in productivity. If this changes, expect higher rates from the Bank of England next year. Just two things will keep the Bank from hiking again – further signs of a significant economic slowdown in the US, and a collapse in our own domestic consumption. For choice I still lean towards expecting another hike, early in 2007. But is it just me, or do the shops feel pretty empty this Christmas?

○ ○ ○ ○ ○

2007

Chapter 5
Headwinds facing the US Mortgage Market?

Stefan Isaacs - Monday, February 19th, 2007

US sub-prime mortgages, those mortgages targeted at consumers with impaired or low credit ratings, have been the talk of the bond markets last week. The sub-prime market has grown significantly in the last few years spurred on by favourable circumstances including a falling unemployment rate, generally rising house prices and ever more accommodative lending practices. That willingness amongst lenders to re-finance existing sub-prime mortgages, often on increasingly favourable terms, meant that even those homeowners who found themselves in real financial difficulty were often able to re-finance. However, that situation has now changed. With existing and new home sales down significantly year on year in 2006 rapid house price appreciation is no longer a source of ready funds for distressed homeowners. Given the general wider strength of the US economy the increase in delinquencies to levels not seen since mid 2003 is a cause for concern. The most recent data has sub-prime loan delinquencies (loans 60 or more days past due or in foreclosure) running at around 12.5%.

Whilst the uptick in delinquencies has been only too apparent in the ABX indices (the riskiest portion rated by Moody's & S&P fell from a price of 96 at the start of the year to 87 on the 15th February, these indices essentially reference sub-prime mortgage debt) the wider impact on the bond markets has been limited. The reason for this is the belief that the issues that are currently plaguing the sub-prime mortgage market are not a symptom of a wider consumer credit problem, that growth remains fairly strong and that the banks involved can fairly comfortably swallow the associated losses. True, delinquency rates on other types of consumer lending are low by historical standards and the larger sub-prime lenders such as Wells Fargo, HSBC, New Century & Countrywide can afford to swallow the associated losses (as you'd expect their equity performance has suffered) concerns remain. Principally I believe there is an obvious danger in assuming that the liquidity this market has enjoyed will be ever present. Sub-prime mortgages typically enjoy a 'low' fixed rate for a couple of years and then jump to levels of around 13%. Should borrowers find in a few years time that they are unable to re-finance (tighter lending standards on the back of this recent scare?) we could well see delinquencies rise significantly and I'm not so sure the wider bond markets could remain quite so sanguine.

Chapter 6
Record bank lending – inflationary pressures remain

Richard Woolnough - Wednesday, February 21st, 2007

Not since I began working in the City in the mid 1980s can I remember seeing an economic data release come out so many billions higher than market expectations. Yesterday morning, it was announced that so-called M4 lending, which is the amount of money in loans that is pumped out by banks, jumped to a new record of £31.7bn in January. A survey of economists had predicted a figure of £11.8bn – that's a difference of £19.9bn! To put this figure in perspective, M4 lending in January was larger than in the whole of 1994. Yesterday the Bank of

England also announced that M4 money supply growth, which is the broadest measure of UK money supply including notes and coins in circulation and bank deposits, rose 13% from a year earlier, ahead of the 12.7% survey prediction and only slightly below the 16 year high of 14.4% that was reached last autumn.

Gilts were marginally damaged by these figures, but why did the bond market not sell off by more? Two answers spring to mind – firstly, complacency; and secondly, the focus on money supply is nowhere near as strong now as it was a couple of decades ago, when the government used to target the money supply in an effort to control inflation.

There is no doubt that in the long run, increases in money growth are more often than not associated with increases in inflation. One of Milton Friedman's two most famous quotes was that "inflation is always and everywhere a monetary phenomenon" (the other quote being "there is no such a thing as a free lunch", which is something I don't entirely agree with!).

The Bank of England recognises this link between money supply and inflation, since contained within the last inflation report were the words "strong money growth may be associated with greater spending on goods and services, or upward pressure on asset prices, posing an upside risk to inflation. To the extent that people recognise this, strong money growth may also prompt them to raise their expectations of future inflation".

But the extent to which money supply growth causes inflation is the subject of an economic debate that has been raging for centuries. I don't want to go into this here, although it is definitely worth mentioning that the money supply clearly plays a role in Mervyn King's mind. In "No inflation, no money – the role of money in the economy" , a paper he wrote while Deputy Governor of the Bank of England in 2002, he concludes:

"My own belief is that the absence of money in the standard models which economists use will cause problems in future, and that there will be profitable developments from future research into the way in which money affects risk premia and economic behaviour more generally. Money, I conjecture, will regain an important place in the conversation of economists."

If the Governor of the Bank of England cares about money lending and money supply growth, then so do I. Yesterday's data releases reinforce my view that the Bank of England will have to hike rates twice more, and possibly by more than that.

Chapter 7
Codswallop – AAA ratings all round

Stefan Isaacs - Wednesday, February 28th, 2007

The credit rating agency Moody's this week released the initial output from its widespread review of the banking sector. Whilst the expected outcome had been for a number of banks to benefit from upgrades to their ratings, the market was taken aback by the initial set of rating revisions. The process is set to take place over seven weeks and will cover approximately 1,000 deposit taking banks in over 90 countries. A link to the report is here (free registration is required).

The initial release on the 26th February saw banks in the Nordic region receive upgrades by as many as four or five notches, some to Moody's' highest rating of AAA, ranking them alongside sovereign bond issuers such as the UK, Germany and the US. Moody's' rationale is predicated upon its new Joint Default Analysis (JDA) approach. Moody's claim that "banks will receive national government support, as well as other major forms of external support such as parental support and support from regional and local governments and cooperative and mutualist groups" which have led to the rethink.

The reaction to the upgrades has been twofold. Firstly as you'd expect, those banks so far benefiting from upgrades have seen the value of their bonds rise in response. Secondly, Moody's have come in for a great deal of criticism. Many investors have questioned the lack of transparency in the new process. It had previously been believed that Moody's were already factoring in state and/or parental support. Investors have questioned for example whether a country such as Iceland (with a population similar in size to Hull, and an economy based around cod) has the ability to support banks which have liabilities three times the nation's Gross Domestic Product. The new process has also made it far more difficult to distinguish between banks on a credit fundamental basis given the added parental/governmental factor.

The ongoing process is expected to lead to further upgrades, further confusion and no doubt further criticism. One disgruntled bond trader has created this clip. Warning – may only be funny to bond geeks.

Chapter 8
Icelandic farce continues

Richard Woolnough - Friday, March 16th, 2007

Fitch ratings agency, whose note on Iceland last year originally kicked off the Icelandic banking crisis, yesterday downgraded Iceland's government bonds from AA- to A+. The Icelandic krona fell 1% against the sterling on the news. Fitch said that "the downgrade reflects new data on the balance of payments and the international investment position that points to a material deterioration in Iceland's external balance sheet, amplifying concerns about external debt sustainability" and that the highly leveraged Icelandic economy was "poorly positioned to surmount a prolonged bout of global risk aversion and/or higher international interest rates".

The downgrade may in part be Fitch highlighting Moody's incompetence (Moody's controversially upgraded Iceland's banks to AAA on the basis that they would be bailed out by Iceland's government), but there is no doubt that Iceland's incestuous economy faces great challenges ahead. The Central Bank of Iceland has hiked interest rates from 5.3% in mid 2004 to 14.25% in order to apply the brakes to its overheating economy. Further rate hikes are probably necessary to slow the economy, where inflation reached a peak of 8.6% in August last year.

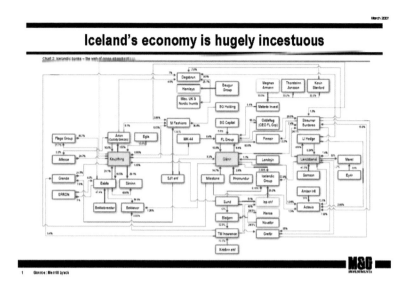

A slowing economy would be very bad news for Iceland's banks (see above Iceland's complicated bank structure). Iceland's three main banks own a large slug of Iceland's companies, and these companies in turn have significant interests in each other. The huge degree of cross ownership is clearly a substantial economic risk, and within the M&G Optimal Income Fund I have bought protection on bonds issued by Kaupthing, one of the "big three" banks exposed to this risk.

Chapter 9
Credit must go to Gordon Brown

Richard Woolnough - Monday, March 26th, 2007

The Financial Times last week ran a story entitled "The City must give credit where it is due", and I think they're right. In my opinion, Gordon Brown has done an excellent job as Chancellor of the Exchequer. Like him or loathe him, the figures really do speak for themselves.

The Chancellor has consistently stated that his number one aim is to maintain and entrench economic stability in the UK. The figures show that since 1997, UK economic growth has been the least volatile of all 28 countries in the OECD. The UK economy hasn't grown the fastest over the period – which is not a surprise considering the OECD includes countries such as Slovakia and South Korea – but it has been a clear leader in terms of stability. Gordon Brown's unerring knack of predicting UK economic growth (predictions that have usually been well wide of those by the City's best paid economists) has been particularly impressive.

While there have been accusations of goalpost shifting regarding the "Golden Rule", the fact is that Gordon Brown has made a better meal of balancing the books than any other chancellor in UK history (only Roy Jenkins, in 1967-1970 came close, and his politically unpopular attempt to run a balanced budget contributed to Ted Heath's surprise election victory in 1970). The UK budget is currently on track to remain balanced over the current economic cycle, and is forecast to move from a deficit of 0.7% of GDP this year to a surplus of 0.2% of GDP in 2008-09 (and remain in surplus thereafter).

Government spending will have to fall if the government is to meet these targets. The government managed to ride out the global slowdown of 2000-02 by increasing spending from 35.1% in 1999-2000 to 39.1% last year, but spending is forecast to fall to 38.3% by 2011-12, fractionally lower than when Labour came to power in 1997.

What does this mean for bond markets? Government borrowing must fall, and since government borrowing is funded by gilt issuance, new issuance of government bonds must fall.

The area of the market that will benefit the most will be long dated gilts. Over the past five years, the surge in government spending has been funded largely by long dated gilt issuance, but the long end has still managed to outperform short and medium dated maturities thanks to pension funds' insatiable appetite. I expect long dated gilts to reap the benefits of the removal of this supply overhang.

Chapter 10
Inflation breaches the Government's target
Mervyn King writes letter to explain why

Jim Leaviss - Tuesday, April 17th, 2007

For the first time since it was granted independence in 1997, the Bank of England's Monetary Policy Committee has had to write an open letter to the Chancellor explaining why inflation has breached the government's target. CPI inflation rose by 3.1% year-on-year in March, more than 1% away from the 2% level. This was up from 2.8% in February. The drivers of this unexpected increase were food, non-alcoholic drinks, furniture and household goods. The RPI print was even higher, at 4.8%, thanks to rising house prices and mortgage interest payments which are not included in the CPI target. Fortunately the bulk of this year's pay round – which tends to focus on RPI as a benchmark – has already gone though, at modest levels of increases. Nevertheless today's numbers make further UK rate rises a certainty, and short dated gilts have sold off heavily this morning.

You can read Governor Mervyn King's letter to the Chancellor, and Gordon Brown's response on the Bank of England's and the HM Treasury's website. In brief, King states that inflation is higher than expected due to domestic energy price hikes, and a weather related global food price hike. However he states that this only explains around half of the problem and that money and credit growth are growing too strongly, and capacity issues are growing – these, to some extent, were within his remit to control, whereas the oil and food prices issues were external shocks. So is he admitting that he should have set a tighter policy? No – he talks a lot about lags in policy setting, and about unforeseen volatility in the inflation numbers, as well as other temporary factors. In particular he expects household gas and electricity prices to fall back later this year, bringing inflation back within target. He says that the MPC will assess these inflation numbers at its May meeting (flagging a hike then). His final quote is probably quite reasonable – "when the MPC was set up in 1997, the chances of going almost ten years without an open letter being triggered seemed negligible". And the Bank has done a good job – but whereas inflation was consistently below the government's target in the first half of the decade since independence (under Lord George), it has been stubbonly above it in more recent years.

Chapter 11
SLM Corp – A Sign of Things to Come?

Stefan Isaacs - Tuesday, April 17th, 2007

SLM Corporation, commonly known as Sallie Mae, announced yesterday that it is to be sold to a group of investors led by two private equity houses for $25 billion. The two private equity players will own 50.2% of the business with Bank of America & JP Morgan Chase splitting the balance. The two banks have also agreed to put a whopping $200 billion in backup financing in place over the next five years. So is this just another in a long line of leveraged buyouts seen recently in the US? Well not exactly.

You see Sallie Mae provides government guaranteed and private student loans in the US, which means that it resides in the financial sector. So what you ask? Well, financial companies were considered less likely candidates for an LBO than most other sectors. In fact many considered them almost LBO proof. The thinking goes that the financial business is either too cyclical to support aggressive leverage and/or requires access to cheap funding that is the preserve of a more conservative balance sheet. In other words, people have always believed that financial companies need an investment grade credit rating to do business – i.e. a minimum of a BBB rating, and usually at least A. However, there are a number of examples within the sector where LBOs have been achieved and we believe that we could potentially see more in the future. Clearly the largest of the banks may yet prove too big to LBO but those finance companies with depressed share prices (pre LBO SLM Corp share price had fallen 12% YTD) will undoubtedly come under ever greater scrutiny from a private equity community with very deep pockets. So far bondholders in financial companies could have been fairly relaxed about the chances of their bonds getting junked (in other words their ratings cut to BB or below) – not any more.

Chapter 12
International housing market looks jittery

Richard Woolnough - Wednesday, April 25th, 2007

There was further evidence of a slowdown in the US housing market yesterday, as sub-prime mortgage woes contributed to existing home sales falling 8.4% in March, the largest monthly decline since records began in 1999 and significantly below expectations of a 4.3% decline.

The US is not the only country with a wobbly housing market – Spanish house price inflation slowed to an annual rate of 7.1% in Q1, down from 9.1% in Q4 2006. The Bank of Spain has previously said that the Spanish housing market is 40% overvalued and fears of impending doom saw Spanish real estate stocks close as much as 25% lower yesterday. Concerns have spread to the Spanish banking sector, much of which is hugely levered and has considerable exposure to the real estate sector. Meanwhile, Denmark yesterday announced that house price inflation slowed to 1.2% in Q1, a fairly worrying slowdown considering that Denmark had the strongest house price inflation in Europe in both 2005 (20%) and 2006 (20%).

So far there is no evidence of a slowdown in the UK housing market, and the pressure is therefore on the Bank of England to raise rates. But if housing markets around the world continue to stall then global growth will inevitably follow, and this is something we are keeping a keen eye on.

Chapter 13
Scottish independence – would I end up with Scottish gilts? And would I want `em?

Jim Leaviss - Monday, April 30th, 2007

The pollsters reckon that the Scottish National Party will become the single biggest party in Scotland following the elections later this week. This has understandably led to thoughts that a subsequent referendum could result in a majority in favour of leaving the 300 year union between England and Scotland, and have Scotland becoming an independent state within the EU. This led me to think that the billions of pounds of UK government gilts we own in our portfolios might end up being something very different by the time that they mature. As in any divorce, a breakup of the UK will lead to some redistribution of assets and liabilities (I remember the Czech and Slovak governments arguing over who got the tastiest embassies after their separation). Scotland accounts for around 9% of the UK population, and slightly less as a share of GDP, so would 9% of my gilt portfolio turn into Scottish Government Bonds overnight? And would Scotland adopt the Euro, in which case the yield on those Scottish bonds might fall from over 5% (UK 10 year yields) to 4.3% (EU 10 year yields), or would they create their own Scottish Pound, in which case you might guess that yields would rise on account of newness and uncertainty. On a stand alone basis would the Scottish economy be AAA rated like the UK? Would Scottish ratings be helped by oil revenues? Or would they suffer to reflect a mediocre GDP record and static population growth? I don't know the answers, but I'll want to as the prospect of independence grows. In the meantime, William Hill is offering 101 to 1 on Scottish independence by May 2012, which might be worth a very small wager. 11 to 1 by 2057 sounds a much better proposition, although 50 years worth of inflation and counterparty risk probably erode the attractiveness of the bet.

Chapter 14
A 1 in 3 chance of US recession – is Greenspan right?

Jim Leaviss - Wednesday, May 23rd, 2007

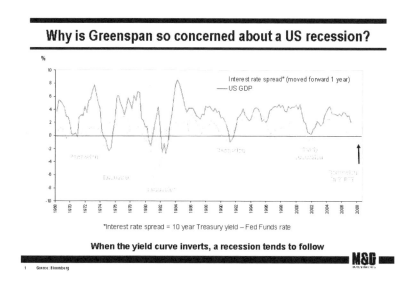

Why is Greenspan so concerned about a US recession?

Interest rate spread* (moved forward 1 year)
—— US GDP

*Interest rate spread = 10 year Treasury yield – Fed Funds rate

When the yield curve inverts, a recession tends to follow

M&G

Source: Bloomberg

We've talked a fair bit about the possibility of a significant US slowdown over the course of the next twelve months. Now that we've cracked the dark arts of posting charts on our blog, I thought it's worth showing you the simple yield curve analysis that lies behind both Greenspan's, and the current Fed's, thinking. History shows us that when long term bond yields in the US fall below the Fed Funds rate, the US economy slips into recession within a year. The chart above shows this happening in the early 1970s, mid 1970s, early 1980s, early 1990s, and in 2001 (marked as "Nearly Recession" on the chart – we didn't see negative GDP growth, but US recessions are "declared", like Port vintages rather than scientifically measured!). It's been a very accurate predictor of economic weakness, and the bad news is that we've seen an inversion in the yield curve for several months now, implying that there will be a recession next year.

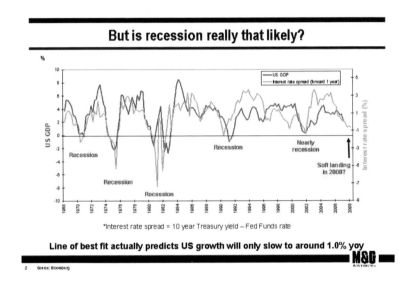

But is recession really that likely?

*Interest rate spread = 10 year Treasury yield – Fed Funds rate

Line of best fit actually predicts US growth will only slow to around 1.0% yoy

Our next chart is less pessimistic though – it plots the "line of best fit" for the relationship between growth and the yield curve. On this measure you might expect a soft landing in the US next year, with annual GDP growth of perhaps 1%. This is still way below trend growth though (3-4%?), and as such an output gap is opening up – we have already had almost a year of sub-trend growth in the States. In my view this growing output gap is disinflationary (actual growth being below the potential of the economy), and helps explain why core US inflation data has been well behaved lately, and should remain subdued going forwards. This is better news for government bonds, which have been in a bear market.

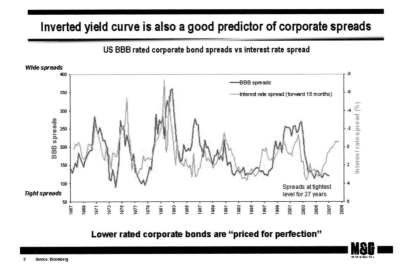

Inverted yield curve is also a good predictor of corporate spreads

US BBB rated corporate bond spreads vs interest rate spread

Lower rated corporate bonds are "priced for perfection"

Where we worry most is in the yield curve's predictive powers for credit spreads. Our third chart shows that BBB rated bonds (the lowest rated investment grade companies) are paying the lowest premium over government bonds for nearly 30 years. If we show the yield curve chart against this (and inverted) we can see that the historical relationship has broken down aggressively in the last couple of years. Given the yield curve is suggesting an economic slow down, we would expect credit spreads to have widened to reflect a riskier world and future higher default rates – but they haven't done so. The simple model might predict that corporate bond yields should be around 200 bps more than government bond yields, rather than just over 100 bps as they are right now. As a result we think lower rated corporate bonds are expensive, perhaps simply reflecting an excess of demand (for example from the CDO market) in a period when we feel monetary policy has been too loose. Our funds are defensive in terms of our credit exposure – the yield curve has a good predictive track record, and it feels right to draw in one's horns and take some chips off the table (to mix metaphors) at this time of the economic cycle.

Chapter 15
"How I saved the global economy" by Alan Greenspan

Jim Leaviss - Friday, August 31st, 2007

We have just 17 days to wait till the publication of Alan Greenspan's autobiography, "The Age of Turbulence: Adventures in a New World". It's 544 pages long, so hopefully nobody will buy it for me for Christmas, but from the synopsis that's been released we learn what a great job he did of saving the world:

> *"The most remarkable thing that happened to the world economy after 9/11 was …nothing. What would have once meant a crippling shock to the system was absorbed astonishingly quickly, partly due to the efforts of the then Chairman of the Federal Reserve Board, Alan Greenspan. The post 9/11 global economy is a new and turbulent system – vastly more flexible, resilient, open, self-directing, and fast-changing than it was even twenty years ago."*

Events of the last couple of months show that the economy is a little less flexible and resilient than claimed – and many would argue that the huge imbalances in the western economies have resulted from Greenspan's actions at the Fed. Whilst rates needed to come down post 9/11 and the bursting of the tech bubble, they were then kept at emergency levels for far too long. The Fed Funds rate was kept at 2% or below from September 2001 all the way through to November 2004, yet US growth had recovered significantly by the third quarter of 2003 and was probably well above trend by early 2004. This mispricing of the cost of money simply created another bubble, this time in residential property, as well as increasing the attractiveness of leverage in the financial sector. The unwind has only just begun. Bernanke got the hospital pass, Greenspan got the book deal.

Chapter 16
Beware of falling rocks

Richard Woolnough - Monday, September 24th, 2007

The Bank of England's controversial decision to bail out Northern Rock depositors, which was probably necessary to prevent a UK banking sector collapse, has done very little to halt the slide in Northern Rock's equity price and for good reason. The Bank of England has been clear that its rescue is only a temporary measure, and Northern Rock's potential to write new business and take deposits is therefore very limited, meaning that Northern Rock's business model is no longer valid.

Financial bonds have significantly underperformed other investment grade corporate bonds over the past few months, with Tier 1 bank bonds (which are subordinated bank bonds) performing worse than single-B rated bonds during the credit sell off. The average spread on UK Tier 1 bank bonds, which are rated about A- on average, is 236 basis points at the time of writing. Tier 1 banks are trading at a level you'd expect to see from a junk bond rather than a bank.

Does this mean that Tier 1 financials are now the deal of the decade? I don't think so. All Tier 1 bonds have a call option, whereby banks have the option to buy the bonds back at a set price on a given date in the future. Although this is an 'option' in the literal sense, the banks have previously stated that they **will** call these bonds (call dates are typically 10 years after issue).

But events of the past few months mean that it's not actually in banks' interest to retire existing debt and reissue it, because they will be losing money in the process. Banks will still try to do everything possible to call Tier 1 bonds because the reputational risk will be extremely damaging if they turn around and show two fingers to the markets, but Northern Rock's experience suggests that some banks may not be able to afford to refinance these bonds. And if one large bank elects not to call Tier 1 bonds, and is not punished excessively by the market, then other banks could well follow suit. Bonds that were previously thought to have maturities in 5 or 10 years could suddenly become undated, which greatly increases the risk of holding them.

The problems don't stop there. Have a look at the chart on Northern Rock's capital structure (which is from June, before the BofE lifeline). At the top of the capital structure sit investors in senior secured paper, who are the first in line to get paid if the company runs into trouble. Equity investors sit at the very bottom. If Northern Rock's position deteriorates further, the bank could first of all stop paying dividends to its equity investors. After that it is allowed to stop paying dividends to preference share holders. If it stops paying dividends to pref holders, it can then renege on its interest payments to Tier 1 bond holders.

So Tier 1 bonds, which were seen as a one way bet a couple of years ago (0.8% premium for bank bonds? Fantastic!) could suddenly go from being low risk, highly rated bonds with just 5 years to maturity, to being perpetual bonds with no maturity that don't pay any interest. Is a 2.36% premium over government bonds enough to compensate me for this not-insignificant risk? Not in my opinion.

As an aside, it's interesting to note that debt and deposits combined form £107.7bn of Northern Rock's capital structure, while equity makes up £1.9bn, just 1.7% of the total, as at the end of June. Some people might understandably find equities more exciting, but as the recent credit crunch has demonstrated, the importance of what goes on in the bond and money markets cannot be understated.

Chapter 17
Merrill Lynch reveals huge write-downs

Ben Lord - Wednesday, October 24th, 2007

In its Q3 results, Merrill Lynch today reported a write-down of $7.9bn across CDOs and US sub-prime, significantly greater than the $4.5bn disclosed in its earnings pre-release. Net revenues fell by 94% on Q3 2006 – as the joke goes, you can only lose 100% of your revenues, although this wasn't far off. Both S&P and Fitch cut Merrill Lynch's rating from AA- to A+, with S&P's analyst describing the results as 'startling'. Merrill Lynch's share price was at one point 10% down, before staging a slight recovery.

If you're an equity investor, investment banks have been a bad bet over the past few months (with the exception of Goldman Sachs). The Dow Jones is close to record highs, and yet the share prices of Bear Stearns and Merrill Lynch are 30% below the highs hit earlier this year. JP Morgan and Morgan Stanley are 15% down.

From what we've seen in the fixed income markets over the past few months, we think that the banks' problems are going to get worse before they get better. In the leveraged loan market, for example, investment banks have struggled to shift loans from the jumbo LBOs off their balance sheets following the repricing of credit risk over the past few months. They have now started to have some success, but they are doing this by selling the bonds at discounts just to shift them before the end of the year and the annual reporting season.

One saving grace for investment banks is that they offer a range of services that cover different markets through the economic cycle. If M&A activity grinds to a halt, they can afford to take the hit, fire most of their M&A team, and employ a new department in, say, distressed debt. This is a luxury that companies like Northern Rock (and to a lesser extent, Alliance & Leicester and Bradford & Bingley) don't have. As Richard argued on this blog last month, Northern Rock is in serious trouble because its entire business model is no longer valid.

Oh, and yet more terrible US housing data just out – existing home sales were -8.0% in September, way below expectations of -4.5% and the worst month since records began in 1999.

Chapter 18
It don't matter if you're black or white?

Mike Riddell - Thursday, November 8th, 2007

We've written a lot about the US sub-prime crisis and some of the very nasty housing stats coming out of the US, but sometimes it takes 'real life' examples to realise just how bad the situation has become for US homeowners, and how much worse it can get. There was an excellent piece on the BBC website earlier this week, which focused on Cleveland, Ohio – "the sub-prime capital of the United States", where one in ten homes are now vacant.

It's not just an economic problem, it's also become a very serious social problem. The BBC's article includes a map of Cleveland, illustrating which areas of the city have the highest concentration of sub-prime borrowing. You can cross-reference this against the areas with the highest black population, and the correlation is extremely close. The same applies across the whole of the US. For example, nearly half of the entire black community who bought a house in 2005 and 2006 in Atlanta took out a high interest mortgage, versus just 13% for white home buyers.

There is a lot of debate about this racial disparity. Some say financial institutions have targeted ethnic groups, but most likely it is because black and hispanic people earn less on average and are therefore more likely to be sub-prime borrowers. Either way, the US sub-prime crisis could turn out to be one of the biggest drivers of racial inequality in US history.

On a slightly lighter tone, Michael Jackson might be told to 'Beat It' after he appeared in Santa Barbara's Foreclosure Detail Report. Michael Jackson has missed over $200,000 in mortgage payments on a $23m loan for his Neverland Ranch. It's not just the sub-prime borrowers who are falling 'off the wall'.

Chapter 19
Now we know how much 'AAA' rated CDOs are really worth

Mike Riddell - Friday, November 9th, 2007

Carina Ltd, a CDO managed by State Street, is being liquidated after the credit quality of its collateral fell below predetermined levels, allowing senior note holders to force a fire-sale of assets. Carina was originally a $1.5bn CDO when it was launched in September 2006, and is the first CDO to begin unwinding since the credit crunch began. The rating on an AAA rated portion of the CDO was downgraded 18 notches by S&P, taking the rating to CCC-.

S&P has been informed of the default of 13 other CDOs. The dumping of assets on the market should see prices in all forms of structured credit continue to spiral downwards, which will inevitably cause spreads in the conventional corporate bond and high yield bond market to widen in sympathy.

Chapter 20
Anarchy in the UK – it's coming sometime, maybe

Jim Leaviss - Tuesday, November 13th, 2007

Not another bearish comment on the financial system, it's just that I went to see the Sex Pistols at Brixton Academy last night, and that song was their encore. They were ace, but now I can't hear. Back when they got famous in inflation-ridden 1976, oil was only $50 a barrel in today's money. Them were the days.

OK – I can't resist. Let's turn it into a bearish comment on the UK financial system. There's a much quoted fact that modern society is just three missed meals from anarchy. I tried to track down the source of this wisdom – Marx perhaps, or Che Guevara? It turns out that it comes from here: "They say that every society is only three meals away from revolution. Deprive a culture of food for three meals, and you'll have an anarchy". Arnold Rimmer, from sci-fi comedy Red Dwarf. How far away were we from a full blown banking collapse in mid September? I think that if the Government hadn't guaranteed all Northern Rock deposits when it did, late on Monday 17th, we would have been there. The share prices of two similarly funded mortgage banks had started to slide dramatically, which would have been negatively reported in the next day's press, leading to queues in all directions on the UK's high streets for the rest of the week. And queuing was not an irrational response – as my dad likes to say whenever there's talk of a petrol blockade, "if you're going to panic, panic early", and off he drives to the BP garage. Deposit protection is of course limited, and who knows how long it would take to get your money back? For all the criticism the authorities have had thrown at them recently, they averted a run on the UK banking system. They did the right thing.

Which brings me to my next thought – what happens when a population loses faith in the banking sector? What happens if something like the run on Northern Rock happens again? Well we saw what happened in Japan over the last decade following the bubble bursting there, with its associated banking crisis – people put their money into the state backed Japan Post savings bank. As a result Japan Post became the largest holder of savings in the world, and accounted for 25% of all Japanese household assets. Japan Post invested a lot of these savings into Japanese Government Bonds (JGBs) and yields on those assets fell to around 0.5%. We have already started to see something similar happen here – National Savings & Investments reported record inflows around the time of the Northern Rock crisis, with sales doubling or trebling for many of its products. Sales of such products help finance the government's budget deficit, so as a result gilt issuance will be lower than it would have been. If it does happen again, expect massive inflows into these 100% safe products, and into AAA rated gilts. And watch gilt yields fall, and fall, and fall…

Chapter 21
The global economy has reached a 'Minsky Moment'

Stefan Isaacs - Thursday, November 15th, 2007

US economist Hyman Minsky came to the public eye after his model on asset bubbles unerringly predicted the boom and bust of tech stocks (unfortunately Minsky didn't live to see his fame – he died in 1996). The credit bubble deflation that global financial markets are now facing is following a similar pattern.

Minsky's underlying theory was that stability breeds instability. Long periods of economic stability result in investors taking more and more risk. As demand for risky assets increases, there is a compression in the risk premium. Leverage begins to grow in predictable stages as investors take advantage of easy credit access to borrow excessively, and end up overpaying for assets.

Minsky believed there were three types of borrower, who are increasingly risky in nature. Hedged borrowers are able to meet debt payments from cash flows. Speculative borrowers can meet interest payments, but have to keep rolling the debt over to pay back the original loan (think Northern Rock). Ponzi borrowers (named after the Ponzi pyramid scheme in the US) aren't able to repay interest or the original debt, and rely on rising asset prices to allow the debt to be refinanced (think sub-prime borrowers). The longer economic stability lasts, the greater the portion of Ponzi borrowers. Financial institutions react to stability and low risk premiums by increasing leverage and devising ways of getting around regulations in an effort to drive profits higher (think of off-balance sheet financing such as SIVs).

The 'Minsky Moment' comes when risk appetite goes into reverse. "This is likely to lead to a collapse of asset vales", wrote Minsky. It looks like May this year marked the inflexion point, when the spread (i.e. excess yield over government bonds) available on US and European high yield bonds reached all-time lows. Spreads have widened considerably over the past few months, but as we've argued on this blog, we think the repricing of risk has only just begun. The Ponzi sub-prime borrowers have already been hit, but the speculative borrowers are only starting to be hit, and the hedged borrowers are still sitting comfortably. We're still at the early stages of forced selling, as CDOs liquidate, hedge funds unwind, and investors reduce leverage.

Many thanks to George Magnus, Senior Economic Adviser at UBS, who has written a number of pieces on Minsky this year.

Chapter 22
The People's Post Office

Jim Leaviss - Tuesday, November 27th, 2007

A couple of weeks ago I wrote about the possibility of the Post Office and National Savings taking a larger and larger share of the UK's savings if confidence in the banking sector continues to wobble (see this link http://bit.ly/u0uQTd). In the Japanese recession their Post Office at one stage held 25% of all the world's savings! The weekend press has been full of adverts for the "People's Post Office", offering an interest rate of 6% – "Let's see the high street beat that one", they boast. The Post Office is 100% government owned, so you might think that your deposits are 100% risk free. Sadly this doesn't seem to be the case, and your money is actually being put into an account "provided by Bank of Ireland". This isn't intended to be a comment on the creditworthiness of that institution in particular – I would be concerned if it was any institution other than HM Government. The Bank of Ireland is AA rated at the senior level, but its borrowing costs have risen steeply in the recent credit crisis as the market worries about the state of the Irish property market. Its 5 year credit default swaps (insurance premium against default risk) have risen from just 10 bps per year in June, to over 90 bps now. If the government wishes to outsource the management of the Post Office savings account to a third party it should add its own guarantes for capital, interest and liquidity to prevent even the whiff of losses to depositors. Could the UK economy cope with rolling news coverage of long winding queues outside the Post Office (insert gag here about there already being long winding queues at every Post Office)? The government should offer a lower rate than the market on its savings products, but give absolute security of investment. As a comment left by a reader on the blog that I wrote about NS&I noted, the government is offering the highest cash ISA rate in the market, for the highest level of security. How can that work without crowding out the banking sector?

A digression – a colleague popped into a certain high street bank last week to pay in a cheque. As he queued for a cashier, a salesperson went up and down the line offering customers unsolicited information about taking out buy-to-let mortgages. They used to say that for short-memoried bankers "never again" meant seven years. Is it now less than seven weeks?

Chapter 23
Unfit for human consumption

Jim Leaviss - Thursday, November 29th, 2007

I enjoyed this letter which was printed in the Times last Saturday.

"Sir, The selling and buying of Northern Rock mortgages between banks reminds me of a wartime story. It involved the busy exchange of corned-beef between black-marketeers.

One purchaser complained that the beef he had just bought was unfit for human consumption. He was told that the beef was not intended for human consumption, but for trading purposes only.

N.ELLIOTT

Stockton-on-Tees"

The strains in the money market persist. In the UK, the focus for bank treasurers is to make sure they have liquidity over year end. This has pushed up interbank interest rates way above the Bank of England's official rate of 5.75%. The forward cost of money over New Year is 7.23% (one month rate, one month forward), nearly 1.5% above the Bank rate. Good news for those who are long of cash (money market funds for example) but otherwise a drag on economic growth – and remember that corporate loan rates are fixed from these interbank rates too.

○ ○ ○ ○ ○

2008

Chapter 24
Monoline insurers – what's going on?

Ben Lord - Friday, February 1st, 2008

Monoline insurers have become a very hot topic, and worries about their demise have made financial markets very jumpy. MBIA, the world's largest monoline insurer, yesterday posted a Q4 loss of $2.3bn. Ambac, the second biggest monoline insurer, posted a Q4 loss of $3.3bn last week, and Fitch ratings agency reacted to cutting Ambac's credit rating from AAA to AA (this is a very significant event – see below). Before explaining what's going on with monoline insurers, it's worth explaining what monoline insurers actually do.

The first thing a monoline insurance company needs is a AAA rating (ratings agencies need to be convinced the company has a solid business model, cutting edge risk systems, and sufficient capital for the risks inherent in the business). Then, the monoline insurance company insures a bond holder against the risk of the bond defaulting. If the bond defaults, the monoline insurer continues to pay the coupons of the defaulted entity as if the bond had not defaulted. The monolines' reward for taking this risk is that they receive a slice of the coupon or interest payments that the bond holder receives. The monolines' guarantee means that the bond is now effectively AAA rated, even if it may only have been single-A rated originally. This process is called 'wrapping'.

Monolines started off by wrapping US municipal bonds, local authority bonds or single company bonds. Munis and local authority bonds are attractive to wrap, because they offer a premium over US treasuries (they're not explicitly guaranteed by the US government, and are often rated A and BBB). But as the monoline industry got more competitive and corporate bond spreads tightened, most monolines became more aggressive. Rather than just focusing on quasi-government bonds, monolines started wrapping ever more exotic bonds, to the point that some monoline insurers began wrapping structured credit exposed to the crumbling US sub-prime mortgage market.

That is really how we have ended up where we are today, in a pretty perfect vicious circle: as structured finance deals are downgraded, their mono-line backers have to write down losses and themselves get downgraded. The wrapped CDO holder is now really no better off than the unwrapped CDO holder (in fact he's worse off, as he's paid away an insurance premium to the monoline at every coupon date!).

Monolines very quickly need an injection of capital from somewhere, otherwise they will be downgraded. And if they are downgraded, their business models cease to function (some lower rated monolines do exist, but only by insuring junk bonds rather than AAA rated bonds – after all, who would buy insurance on a AAA rated wrap when the insurance company itself is only 'A' rated?).

If the monoline insurers collapse, then investment banks will be in even deeper trouble than they are today. Many investment banks have bought protection from the monolines so that they can hedge structured credit exposure on their own balance sheets in order to insulate themselves from making losses. But if the monolines go bust, then the investment banks are left with a worthless insurance contract, and a whole lot more exposure to structured credit and sub-prime.

It's not just the investment banks that would be in trouble. Monolines guarantee about $2.4 trillion worth of bonds with their AAA rating, and if the monolines are downgraded, then hundreds of thousands of other bonds would be downgraded too. This would spark a wave of forced selling from investors such as pension funds, and then we would see (yet another) wave of writedowns from the investment banks.

Do we think that the monoline business model will return to its operating state prior to the current crisis? Absolutely not. They are too highly levered, they don't have enough capital for a AAA rating, and they don't have enough capital to provide sufficient protection to investors. Their reputations are in tatters. But will they be allowed to fail totally? We don't think so, because there are plenty of bond holders that have a very clear motivation to ensure that the monolines don't disappear. In a rather bizarre twist, it looks like the investment banks are going to have to club together and rescue the companies from which they've bought insurance. If you like analogies, it's a bit like taking out insurance on your home, only to find that when your house burns down, you have to give the insurance company a load more money to stop it from going bust.

Chapter 25
European recession will put a huge strain on European Monetary Union

Stefan Isaacs - Friday, February 8th, 2008

After a few teething problems, it's not contentious to say that the euro has been a success. Helped by the US dollar's demise, the euro is gradually becoming a rival as the reserve currency of choice for central banks. European unemployment has plummeted, and the European economy probably grew at around 3% last year. Some countries have boomed – Spanish economic growth has averaged about 4% over the past two years, while Ireland has done even better, with growth averaging almost 7% over the past decade. The unemployment rate in Spain 10 years ago was 20%, and it touched 8% last year.

The problem is, however, that some areas of Europe have been far too hot. ECB interest rates may have been about right for Germany or France, but they have definitely not been high enough for countries like Ireland and Spain. As we know so well from the US experience, artificially low interest rates cause asset price bubbles. Spanish and Irish property markets were el scorchio until recently, but the house price chart for Ireland looks uncannily like that of the US

– double digit house price growth from 2000-06, followed by a slump of -7.3% for 2007. Spanish and Irish banks are now in serious trouble due to their huge property exposure.

European economics is about to get very, very political. How will Irish politicians react if the Irish economy enters a depression? Will they sit quietly while the ECB keeps interest rates on hold, and continues its tough talk on anchoring inflation expectations? How will the Irish public react when unemployment surges? Spain's prime minister, Jose Luis Rodriguez Zapatero, kicked things off this week by saying that the ECB will cut interest rates by 0.5% this year. The ECB would have been none too impressed, given its obsession with appearing unified in its rate decisions and its communication to financial markets (Bank of England style voting results are inconceivable).

A big recession in Europe could put the European Monetary Union (EMU) at risk, as leaders accountable for their struggling economies decide that they're better off in control of their own monetary policy.

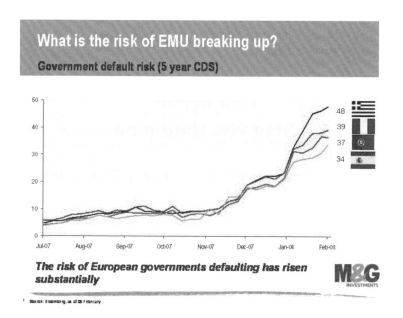

What is the risk of EMU breaking up?

Government default risk (5 year CDS)

The risk of European governments defaulting has risen substantially

This chart is fascinating as it shows that financial markets are starting to consider the potential of EMU breaking apart. If EMU collapsed, you can be sure that countries such as Italy, Greece and Spain would trade at a much wider premium than they do now (particularly if an economic depression in these countries was the reason for EMU falling apart). As the chart shows, the cost of taking out insurance on Greek government bonds defaulting in the next five years is now 0.5% (as shown by 5 year CDS spreads). When the credit crunch began in July 2007, the cost of insurance on Greek government bonds was 0.05%. To put the figure of 0.5% into context, this is where Astrazeneca or Glaxosmithkline 5 year CDS trades right now, and is where Societe Generale senior 5 year CDS traded less than a month ago.

I believe that the risk of EMU collapsing is very small, precisely because the ECB will do anything to stop it from happening. The breakup of EMU will mean the death of the ECB, so it's hardly in their interests. As European economic data continues to weaken over the coming months, I believe the ECB will start to downplay the inflation risks and increase emphasis on downside risks to growth. Then, from the summer, I think they will start a cycle of interest rate cutting. For this reason, I have moved longer duration in the M&G European Corporate Bond Fund, as I believe rates will fall by more than the market is pricing in.

Chapter 26
Stag yes, flation no

Jim Leaviss - Friday, February 22nd, 2008

Markets have rapidly moved towards our long held view that the global economy is slowing aggressively, and that recession is imminent (or already here) in the States. However it seems that the consensus is that this growth slowdown will be accompanied by strongly rising consumer prices – in other words stagflation. I don't believe that's likely. The consequence of a global banking crisis (and that's what this is) is that liquidity is withdrawn from the system, and the availability of credit is significantly reduced – these are not inflationary outcomes. Here's what happened to inflation in the aftermath of banking crises in the last century.

Banking Crisis – *Change in inflation over next two years*

Wall Street Crash (1929) – *Fell from -1% to -10%*

Savings & Loans (early 1980s) — *Fell from 15% to 3%*

Japanese bubble bursting (end 1980s) – *Fell from 3.5% to 1%*

Swedish Banking Crisis (early 1990s) — *Fell from 10% to 2.5%*

Asian Financial Crisis (1997) — *Fell from 4.5% to 1% (Thai data as proxy)*

Global Credit Crunch (2007-?) – ?

Sure, food prices are rising (and will stay high), and oil is $100 a barrel – but the key driver of inflation is the difference between actual growth and the economy's potential growth. As the output gap opens up as growth slows, dis-inflationary pressure builds – there is overcapacity, and no supply of credit. With a combined share of around 15% of the inflation basket, higher food and energy prices will hurt consumers – badly – but unless they can negotiate higher wages in response (unlikely) they'll have to reduce spending elsewhere. Thanks to the credit crunch, borrowing to finance discretionary spending will be more expensive and harder to find. Central banks need not worry about inflation – but they must stop the banking crisis from accelerating. Ben Bernanke knows this, and that's why we could see a 1% Fed Funds rate later this year.

Chapter 27
US housing downturn worst since Great Depression – and getting worse

Mike Riddell - Thursday, February 28th, 2008

Investors are almost becoming blasé to dire US housing market data releases, but the reality is that things are getting worse and worse.

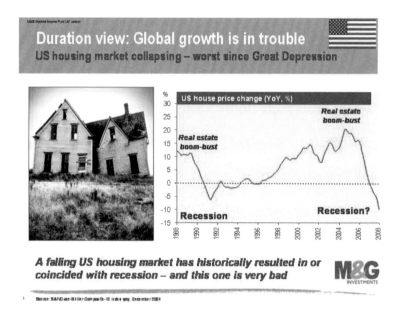

Duration view: Global growth is in trouble
US housing market collapsing – worst since Great Depression

A falling US housing market has historically resulted in or coincided with recession – and this one is very bad

The monthly S&P/Case-Shiller figures that came out on Tuesday showed that the US housing market downturn is now more severe than the one that led to the US recession in 1991. As the chart shows, the S&P/Case-Shiller Index Composite-10 Index fell by 9.8% in the year to the end of December. In Q4, the index fell by 21.0% on an annualised basis. This index starts in 1987 – for a longer history, you need to look at indices such as the catchily-named 'US New One Family Houses Sold Annual Median Year Over Year Price Change'. This index fell 15.1% in the year to the end of January, the biggest fall since records began in 1964.

The excess supply of houses in the market suggests US house prices will continue deflating. The number of US homes for sale rose 5.5% to 4.2 million in January – at the reported sales pace, this represents 10.3 months' supply, just below the record set last October. The months' supply of new homes on the market rose to 9.9, representing the largest housing stock overhang in the US since 1981. US house prices will continue falling until this overhang is significantly reduced.

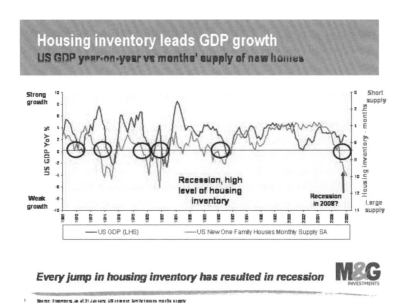

Housing inventory leads GDP growth
US GDP year-on-year vs months' supply of new homes

Recession, high level of housing inventory

Recession in 2008?

Every jump in housing inventory has resulted in recession

Source: Bloomberg, as at 31 January, US one one family houses months supply

This chart shows that the months' supply of new homes is a very good predictor of US recessions. When the months' supply of new homes breaks above 7 months (as shown by the yellow line, inverted on the right hand axis), the economy goes into recession (blue line, left hand axis). A figure of around 10 months' supply suggests the US is about to head into a nasty recession – worse than what we saw in 1991, more akin to 1974-5.

Ben Bernanke yesterday stated that US real GDP has 'slowed sharply since the third quarter', US consumer spending has 'slowed significantly' since the end of 2007, and that labour market conditions have 'softened'. Furthermore, 'the risks to this outlook remain to the downside…the housing market or labour market may deteriorate more than is currently anticipated and that credit conditions may tighten substantially further'. This is a clear indication that the Federal Reserve is prepared to lower interest rates further. The Bank of England now needs to act in a similar manner.

Chapter 28
UK unemployment lowest since the 1970s – watch it rise

Richard Woolnough - Friday, April 18th, 2008

The government's official unemployment rate (which looks just at the number of people claiming benefits) stands at 2.5%, the lowest rate since 1975. The UK unemployment rate under the International Labour Organisation's measure stands at a slightly more realistic 5.2%, which is higher that 2003-06, but still way below the long term historical average.

A widely held view is that the UK economy will be OK, because unemployment is low. This view is misplaced. History suggests that unemployment is a lagging indicator – that is, it's one of the last things to turn in an economic slowdown. What has normally happened in the past is that house prices fall, then consumer spending falls (and economic growth therefore slows), then unemployment rises, and finally inflation starts to fall as spare capacity is created in the economy.

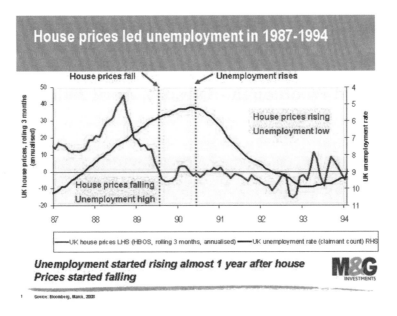

House prices led unemployment in 1987-1994

Unemployment started rising almost 1 year after house Prices started falling

Source: Bloomberg, March, 2008

This graph shows what happened in the UK's last recession. House prices are represented by the blue line, and we've looked at house price changes on a rolling 3 months (and annualised). UK unemployment is the red line, and is plotted against the right hand axis (inverted). Last time around, UK house prices started falling in mid-1989, but unemployment didn't start rising until mid-1990.

Unemployment is a lagging indicator because it takes companies a while to realise that the economy is slowing. Once companies realise this, it then takes them a while to lay people off. So if you want to get an idea of what's going to happen to the UK economy (or indeed the US economy), look at the housing market, not the unemployment rate. Anyone who's focusing on unemployment as a measure of the state of the economy is likely to be well behind the curve

Chapter 29
Food glorious food

Richard Woolnough - Tuesday, April 29th, 2008

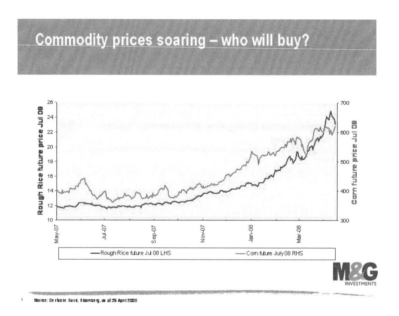

Inflation is public enemy number one for us because it picks our pockets by eroding the real value of our bonds. The latest twist to the inflationary story is the rapid rise in food prices, from the staples of wheat to rice.

Normally central banks can dismiss volatile food prices as temporary, because prices are influenced by random effects such as drought and weather patterns. These temporary blips should not cause second round effects (e.g. higher wages) and therefore shouldn't enter the inflationary food chain – indeed, the Federal Reserve targets core inflation, which strips out food and energy.

However this time around, worrying signs of political interference are resulting in inefficient economic outcomes. The policy response to food shortages in Argentina has been to raise tariffs on exports, meaning that food floods the domestic market and prices stay low. It could be their funeral, as Argentine farmers will likely react by planting less wheat, which drives the price of wheat higher and its supply lower. Shortages will be back soon – Adam Smith would not approve.

Argentina's policy approach is being replicated by other countries around the world (e.g. Russia, Ukraine, China, Serbia, Kazakhstan, Egypt, Vietnam, Indonesia, India, Cambodia and Venezuela). This kind of inflationary protectionism is a worry for bond investors, as food price rises will cease to be short term and temporary, and could instead become long term and permanent. Food forms around half of poorer countries' consumption, and government actions to keep prices down are therefore understandable. But policy makers should be reviewing the situation with regard to the long term implications, rather than doing anything for short term popularity.

Chapter 30
Northern Rock – wishful thinking

Richard Woolnough - Wednesday, August 6th, 2008

It's now been just over a year since the credit crunch began, and there are many indicators of stress out there – equity market falls, credit spreads widening, and collapsing consumer confidence are all things we've focused on over the last year.

Unsurprisingly, the main stress has been in the financial sector, the epicentre of this crisis. This is best typified by the fall of Northern Rock, whose downfall we have chronicled in depth on this blog – for more information see *Not waving but drowning*(Jun 07), *Northern Rock not so solid anymore*(Jul 07), *Beware of Falling Rocks*(Sep 07), *Northern Lights* (Oct 07), a Christmas-themed *Stable conditions*(Dec 07), and most recently *Recovery plan doomed?* (May 08).

Yesterday the government announced that it was injecting £3 billion of its (our) money to subscribe for shares in Northern Rock. Northern Rock's market cap peaked at over £5bn at the beginning of 2007, had fallen to £3.6 billion by

June last year. By the time its shares were delisted, it had a market cap of £380m. Now it's apparently worth almost 10 times what it was valued at in February this year. Wow.

Have things really barely deteriorated from the summer of last year? Have we really seen the most dramatic turn around in corporate history in the last six months? Today, Nationwide announced that UK consumer confidence dropped in July by the most since records began in 2004. It is very wishful thinking to hope that the first time buyer will return, the housing market will not fall, the economy is robust – and most of all – that Northern Rock is worth three billion pounds!

Chapter 31
What will higher government borrowing mean? Steeper gilt yield curves as long dated bonds underperform, and crowding out for the private sector

Jim Leaviss - Wednesday, August 13th, 2008

The newspapers over the past week or so have been full of alleged leaks from the government about fiscal help for the poor British consumer. Ideas floated have included a suspension of stamp duty (although HBOS has pointed out that following the 1991/1992 stamp duty holiday, house prices still fell by 8.3% in that latter year, and transactions fell to their lowest level for 34 years), and a £150 winter fuel bonus for all child benefit recipients. As with the Bush US tax rebates (about $600 per person) earlier this year, the government must hope that a fiscal ease would provide a temporary stimulus to consumption and house prices – although whether propping up property values is a good idea in itself must be open to question even if, unlike in 1991/1992, it were to be successful.

Sadly, whilst I'm all in favour of a bit of Keynesian fiscal stimulus (it eventually proved to be the route out of the Great Depression with the New Deal) the

UK cupboard is bare. Tax revenues will have already started to plunge – for example, the huge fall in property transactions will hit stamp duty receipts (worth £6.4 billion per year in 06/07), and lower prices will take those transactions that do take place into lower tax bands. Other hits to the Exchequer will come from lower VAT receipts as retail sales slow, and weaker capital gains tax receipts as asset prices (shares for example) have come well off their highs. Perhaps only VAT on fuel continues to outperform expectations as petrol prices have rallied, although reported significant falls in volumes may mitigate that too (some suggest demand is down 20% from a year ago).

With economic growth slowing significantly, the other side of the equation, spending, is also likely to move in the wrong direction. Jobless claims have started to increase for the first time in nearly 2 years for example. The worrying thing is that the government's tax and spending estimates are based on growth rate forecasts that look much too high in the current environment, and that certainly don't discount a recession – around 2% in 2008 and 2.5% in 2009. The IMF estimates that actual growth might be around 1.4% this year, and even lower at 1.1% in 2009. The implication is that the UK will struggle to keep its debt as a percentage of GDP ratio below the magic number of 40%. You can read the pessimistic transcript of the IMF's UK economic outlook here.

Lower tax revenues (is a windfall tax on energy companies the only answer?) and higher spending mean that we will get higher government borrowing, and therefore more gilts. As recently as the period 1999 to 2002 the government was repaying the national debt (remember Prudence?), and the UK's Net Debt to GDP ratio was at 30.2%. Net gilt issuance this fiscal year will be £63 billion – the largest ever, and Net Debt to GDP will be 38.5%. So far the gilt market has been remarkably sanguine about this (bar a big sell off on the day that it was reported that Alistair Darling might scrap the "Golden Rule" of borrowing only to invest).

But perhaps the gilt market is right to be relatively relaxed – in fact yields have fallen by over 50 bps at 10 years since June, and gilts have outperformed investment grade bonds and high yield so far this quarter. The last time we had a borrowing scare, in 1993-94 as we were coming out of recession, the gilt market had its best ever year despite the highest ever gilt issuance! In the fiscal year 1993-94 net issuance was £47.5 billion (again, a few years earlier there had been talk of repaying the national debt) and Net Debt to GDP went above 40%. Gilts rallied hard, with 10 year gilt yields falling from 8.25% to nearly 6% by the end of 1993. I worked on the gilt trading desk at the Bank of England at the time, and it felt as if we were issuing stock every day, demand was so strong.

Although gilts rallied hard over that period, the shape of the yield curve changed dramatically. In 1992 the curve had been inverted, with 30 year gilts yielding 50 bps less than 10 year gilts. As concerns about supply grew in 1993, the curve normalised sharply and became steeply upward sloping, with 30 year gilts yielding at least 50 basis points more than at 10 years. As borrowing requirements grew, perceived credit risk of HM Government also grew and a risk premium was demanded by the market to lend at long maturities (governments could default on their debts, or, more likely inflate them away which would have been damaging to holders of long dated gilts).

My colleague Matthew Russell has done some good work on the shape of the yield curve compared with the government borrowing. It shows that given the current level of borrowing, rather than the UK having an inverted yield curve (currently 30 year gilts yield 25 bps less than 10 years) we should have a mildly upward sloping one (perhaps 10 bps positive). If borrowing deteriorates to the level that we expect it to, the yield curve should have a positive slope of more than 50 bps. That's why, despite the ongoing pension fund demand for long dated assets, we would rather take our bullish bond position in the 10 year area of the curve than at the ultra long end of the gilt market which should underperform. For our growing band of American readers, I point you in the direction of some research on the US yield curve which comes to a similarly gloomy conclusion for long dated US bonds, here.

There are some other issues arising from all of this – the most important of which is crowding out. An unrelenting supply of low risk government paper makes it more costly for the corporate sector, with lower credit ratings, to issue debt, thus reducing their profits. Perhaps the best example of crowding out can be seen in the finance pages of your Sunday papers every week. The state-owned Northern Rock is offering interest rates of 6.5% to 7%, with no risk to depositors – this must surely raise the cost of attracting retail deposits for the rest of the struggling UK banking sector. And finally, food for thought – during the long Japanese recession, the world's second largest economy was downgraded from AAA to A2 by Moody's as its borrowing burden reduced its creditworthiness. Could the UK or the US lose their AAA credit ratings?

Chapter 32
When rates get to zero, what happens next? Quantitative easing

Jim Leaviss - Wednesday, October 29th, 2008

Later today the Fed will probably cut US rates by 0.5%, down to 1%. After this we're only a couple of cuts away from a zero percent Fed Funds rate. When rates are at 0%, what can a central bank do to stimulate the economy? Well some possible answers are found in Japan, although with its economy still struggling to print positive growth numbers a full 18 years after its bubble burst, it may not be the best role model. In March 2001, with Japanese short term rates at 0.15%, the Bank of Japan (BoJ) began a quantitative easing programme. With traditional monetary policy no longer effective (the so-called liquidity trap), how could the BoJ stimulate economic activity? It flooded the economy with money by buying financial assets (bills, equity, ABS), and in so-called Rinban operations directly buying Japanese Government Bonds. Rinban operations were designed to make monetary policy effective at longer dated maturities than traditional central bank activities. By buying long dated government bonds the hope was that yields would be pulled down across the curve, and thus reduce borrowing costs for corporates and individuals where loans were benchmarked over government bond yields. The BoJ purchased about $120 billion JGBs per year as part of the plan.

Did it work? Quantitative easing ended 5 years later, with the BoJ having reached its stated aim of returning the economy to inflation (although it did subsequently return to deflation once more). Long dated (20 year) JGB yields did fall too, from about 1.8% in March 2001 to below 1% a couple of years later – but by the time quantitative easing came to an end yields were back up above 2% again, so it's arguable whether this part of the plan was very successful.

Is quantitative easing something that the western economies will consider? Well to some extent it's already here – central banks have turned on the printing presses (the $80 billion to bail out AIG for example), are flooding the money markets with liquidity, and have started to buy financial assets (the equity stakes in banks for example). Purchasing of US Treasury bonds might not be too far behind – and remember that the Fed discussed it once before around the time of the 2002 deflation scare. The FOMC talked about "unconventional measures" including purchasing many types of financial assets (and non-financial too – it's rumoured that they discussed using the secondhand car market as a means of getting cash into the hands of the American public). The June 2002 Fed paper, Preventing Deflation: Lessons from Japan's experience in the 1990s, is well worth revisiting as a route map for the next few years.

And this might well be a story that takes a few years to unfold – it seems difficult for us to believe that the amount of fiscal stimulus, rate cuts, printing press activity and bank recapitalisation thrown at the global economy won't result in a sharp rise in inflation, but the Japan experience shows that even then the most extreme measures can't guarantee that the authorities can generate a bit of lovely inflation.

Chapter 33
The Great Credit Crash

Richard Woolnough - Thursday, October 30th, 2008

Since May 2007, we've seen the Great Credit Crash, with the fastest and sharpest sell off in credit that the modern world has ever seen. In the US, in May 2007, the average BBB corporate bond yielded just 120bps (i.e. 1.2%) over a government bond. The figure was 699bps as at the end of yesterday. BBB rated bonds now yield 10% on average in the US and UK, and almost 9% in Europe. This chart is a good illustration of the severity of the bear market. US BBB spreads have gone from being the tightest in a decade to the widest since July 1932. In fact, spreads were only wider than they are now in May-July 1932, when the excess yield was 720bps.

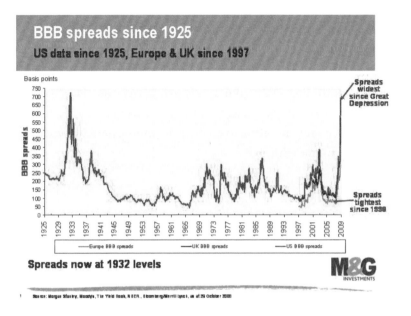

Now clearly the BBB index constituents have changed a bit over the past 76 years, with fewer railroad companies and more PC manufacturers, but what was considered BBB then can be roughly assumed to possess the same credit characteristics as a BBB now. This chart is therefore saying that the credit risk premium is as high now as in the depths of depression in 1932. Put another way, a 7% excess yield means that an investor can afford for 7% of a portfolio of 10 year BBB rated bonds to default every year for 10 years, with a recovery rate of zero pence in the pound, just to break even with the return from a 'risk free' government bond. The investment grade corporate bond market is pricing in a horrific economic scenario.

As readers of this blog will be well aware, we've been very gloomy on the global economy for a couple of years. Judging by where corporate bond yields were until this year, our gloomy economic outlook was not remotely believed by the market. This was particularly true in the high yield (junk) bond market.

But to believe that BBB rated bonds are unattractive now, you have to believe that things are going to be worse than in the 1930s. I believe the global economic outlook is very grim, with the developed world heading for a prolonged, nasty recession, however policy makers have learnt lessons from the 1930s and the many recessions since. Banks are being supported, fiscal stimulus is going to be undertaken and interest rates are being slashed.

For a number of years now, we have thought that the credit risk premium for owning corporate bonds was insufficient, and we positioned our portfolios very defensively in terms of credit risk. We favoured 'AAA' and 'AA' rated bonds over 'A' and 'BBB' rated bonds in investment grade bond funds, and focused our high yield portfolios away from unrewarding risky assets. Now that credit risk premia are extraordinarily high and policy actions are credit positive, we think BBB rated bonds are attractive and it is appropriate to be long of credit risk in investment grade funds.

Chapter 34
Who cares about the Fed – Deutsche Bank didn't call one of their bonds this morning. More carnage for the financial bond sector…

Jim Leaviss - Wednesday, December 17th, 2008

Shock of the morning wasn't the overnight Fed rate cut to zero-ish, nor the acceleration of their Quantitative Easing programme, both of which we'd expected for some time. The shock came with this press release from Deutsche Bank explaining that they wouldn't be calling a Lower Tier 2 (LT2) bank bond. This particular bond, a Euro 1 billion issue, was issued as a 10 year deal, but with a call date after 5 years at the bank's option in January 2009. Historically, these LT2 issues have been called after 5 years, as if not redeemed then the coupon steps up and theroretically makes it expensive funding for the bank. In this instance the coupon moves from 3.875%, to 3 month Euribor (Euro money market rate) +88bps. This currently equates to just over 4%, so is only a minor increase in the interest cost at a time when refinancing bank debt has become extremely expensive. Subordinated Deutsche Bank credit default swaps are trading at 216 bps, so it makes total economic sense for the bank to have left this relative cheap financing outstanding – to issue a brand new LT2 bond might cost Deutsche Bank a coupon of 5.5 – 6%. Euribor +88 bps is inside where the bank could issue even senior debt.

So it made economic sense, but the market was still shellshocked. The price of the bond fell from around 96 to 90 as the market opened, and other LT2 bonds are obviously under pressure too. Many had felt that there would be a credibility issue in not calling debt at this part of the capital structure, and that it might impair a bank's ability to issue cheaply again in the future as well as being seen as a sign of weakness. Now one of the world's biggest banks has taken such a stance however it is likely that every other bank in the world feels able to assess the callability of their outstanding bonds on purely economic grounds (although BNP Paribas did call an LT2 issue today, perhaps before they knew the precedent that DB was setting). All LT2 bonds should therefore be assessed on a yield to maturity (YTM) basis rather than on yield to call (YTC) – in other words the spreads being offered on bank bonds were unrealistically high if quoted to those shorter call dates.

So LT2 bonds are lower this morning, but a bigger hit is likely in the even more subordinated Tier 1 (T1) market. If banks now feel no moral pressure to call the more senior LT2 bonds, they will certainly have no compunction about letting T1 bonds extend maturity – to perpetuity if necessary. And coupled with the fact that many T1 bonds will not be able to pay coupons if the bank isn't paying an equity dividend, many investors are going to be left holding zero coupon perpetual bonds. Bond Maths 101 – the zero coupon perpetual bond is the very worst kind of bond you can own. T1 bonds are 10-12 points lower this morning.

o o o o o

2009

Chapter 35
Moody's predict surge in defaults

Ben Lord - Friday, January 16th, 2009

Moody's this week released their expectations for their global speculative grade default rate. Their default model is now (rather belatedly) indicating that there is to be a surge in defaults through this year, with the global speculative grade (i.e. 'high yield') default rate peaking at 15.4% in November 2009. Moody's use a 12 month trailing default rate, so what they are saying is that 15.4% of the global high yield market will default in the year to the end of November 2009.

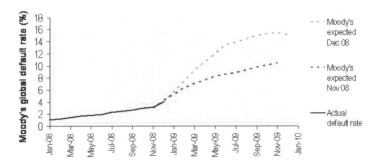

Moody's now expect high yield default rate to hit 15% in 2009

The thing that caught our eyes was the jump in Moody's expected default rate. As this chart shows, only one month previously, Moody's expected a peak of 10%. It's worth adding, though, that November's forecast appeared far too low, especially if you consider that as at the end of November, euro high yield bonds yielded almost 22% more than government bonds, and US high yield bonds yielded 20% more than Treasuries (both figures already implying roughly an annual default rate of 16-17%, and that's assuming a zero recovery rate). In fact, the market doesn't seem too bothered by Moody's updated forecast – high yield spreads have actually tightened a bit since the end of November (the respective figures were 19% for euro HY and 17% for US$ HY as at yesterday).

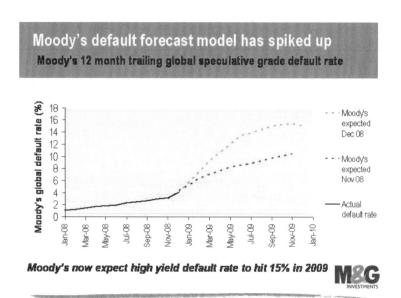

How does a 15% annual default rate compare to the Great Depression? This chart shows Moody's speculative grade default rate going back to 1920. The annual default rate peaked at 16.3% at the end of 1933, so not quite as bad. But the figures aren't really directly comparable. The high yield market didn't exist as such in the 1930s – companies that were rated sub investment grade were 'fallen angels', i.e. companies that were formerly investment grade. Junk companies only started issuing bonds en masse during the Milken years of the 1980s, and the European high yield market didn't start developing until the mid 1990s. A better comparison would be the default rate seen in the early 1990s and particularly 2001-02. We concur with Moody's that default rates should exceed those levels.

But remember, high yield spreads are massively wider than they were in the 1990s and the early 'noughties'. The high market is already pricing in a default rate significantly higher than Moody's is expecting. We are seeing some attractive valuations in the high yield market, and are chipping away at the better quality end where mandates allow. However we do expect defaults to surge, and particularly from the end of 2009 when a lot of high yield names need to refinance. We also expect defaults to be concentrated in companies that were

LBOd in 2006-07 and in cyclical names, and defaults will be very heavy in the poorer rated names (so CCC rated bonds are still basically a no go area for us).

Finally it was interesting to note the Chapter 11 filing of Nortel this week, which was an event that bond markets had priced in since November. Nortel is a company that survived the 2001-02 tech wreck, but hasn't made it this time. This is a good example of why we aren't piling into high yield right now. We remain very bearish on the global economy, with the recession/depression likely to be worse than the early 1990s and obviously much worse than the non-recession of 2001-02. The high yield market hasn't ever been tested by a 1981-82 recession or a 1974, nor even a 1932. So maybe two thirds of the high yield market really could go bust in the next five years (which is about what the bond market's actually pricing in). That said, if you can avoid the companies that do default, then the potential returns are clearly considerable.

Chapter 36
Are the bond vigilantes vigilant enough?

Jim Leaviss - Friday, February 20th, 2009

On the day that the Bank of England started its Quantitative Easing (QE) regime with the purchase of £340 million of commercial paper under the Asset Purchase Facility, it's worth remembering why our blog is called Bond Vigilantes, and ask ourselves whether we need to be baring our teeth a little more.

The term Bond Vigilantes dates from the bond market's aggressive response to President Clinton's attempt to increase the US budget deficit in the 1990s. The Treasury Bond market selloff (leading to rising financing costs for the US) helped to persuade the administration to balance the budget. Clinton's political adviser at the time, James Carville noted "I used to think that if there was reincarnation, I wanted to come back as the president or the pope or as a .400 baseball hitter*. But now I would like to come back as the bond market. You can intimidate everybody".

I would want to come back as Brad Pitt.

Well, with the collapse of the global economy, budget deficits everywhere in the world have been allowed to expand to almost unheard of levels. Government borrowing in the UK will be about 8% of GDP in the next year, the highest in recent history (it hit 7.7% in 1993-94) and our debt to GDP level is quickly heading north of 50%. The Office of National Statistics has declared that the liabilities of the nationalised and part-nationalised UK banks will have to be added to the UK's balance sheet, so we could be nearing 100% pretty imminently. At the same time, the Bank of England is starting to print money and central banks everywhere have added to the government's fiscal stimulus packages with a huge amount of monetary easing (zero interest rate policies). All of this should, on the face of it, be really bad news for investors in government bonds. Fears of a never-ending supply of government bonds, and stories that hyperinflation is on its way, have made many bond investors fearful.

So a good bond vigilante really needs to take a step back from the consensus view that we are going to see a year of weak inflation (perhaps with a period of mild deflation) and then there's a chance that it's Zimbabwe here we come. So what are the theoretical drivers of inflation, and is it possible that the consensus could be very wrong this time?

Are you a monetarist or a Keynesian? Monetarist Milton Friedman popularised what is known as the Quantity Theory of Money. In short, the theory simply reflects the idea that if you print more money, the value of that money is reduced proportionately to the amount of money printed. The equation he used was $MV = PQ$, where M is the amount of money in circulation, V is the velocity of money, P is the price level and Q is the total number of items purchased with the money in circulation. The important thing to note is that there is more than one determinant in the generation of inflation in the economy – the quantity of money is very important, but a rise in this quantity can be offset by a fall in the velocity of money. If money stops moving around the economy (because individuals, banks, and companies are hoarding it) then printing the stuff won't generate inflation. This spreadsheet here allows you to plug in some numbers of your own to estimate what might happen going forwards – I'm using column C, which allows you to input all factors other than inflation. Thinking about the last year, let's say that the broad money supply grew by 17.5% (M4), the velocity of money remained unchanged, and the quantity of goods sold rose by 4.3% (volume of retail sales). This results in annual inflation of 12.66%, but UK CPI in 2008 ended at 3.1%. What change in the velocity of money would therefore result in the actual inflation rate? The answer is that a fall in the velocity of money from 5 to 4.575 results in inflation of 3.1%. This is a slowing in the speed of money going around the economy of 8.5%. Assuming that the other factors remained the same, a decline in the velocity of money of 11% would have led to zero inflation, and anything greater to outright deflation. It therefore follows that even printing money, and doing Ben Bernanke style helicopter drops of dollar bills over the population can't generate inflation unless we go and do something with that cash.

For the Keynesians, I present the output gap theory. The output gap is the difference between the potential growth in an economy (based on factors like demographic growth in the labour market and productivity improvements) and the actual growth. When an economy is growing below trend, it is difficult to generate inflation – too many out of work employees are chasing too few vacancies, and wage growth is stifled. Unused factory capacity, high stocks of inventories, going out of business sales and empty buildings also keep the lid on inflation. Our favourite economist, Paul Krugman published this analysis of the US output gap and its impact on inflation on his NY Times blog a couple of weeks ago (thanks to David Parkinson of RBC for the link). You can see that for every 1% that actual growth falls below potential growth, the inflation rate is reduced by 0.5%. The US Congressional Budget Office is saying that the output gap will be 6.8% over the next two years, which means that the US is staring at a period of deflation, even if you assume that President Obama's fiscal stimulus fills in a third to half of that growth shortfall.

Finally, thinking back to the UK's last period of fiscal indiscipline – the 1993 budget deficit of 7.7% – did the gilt market collapse? Well no. 10 year gilt yields fell from 9.7% to 6.1% – a gigantic rally. A selloff did come, but not until the next year, when the Fed hiked rates – something clearly (and explicitly) not on the cards for some time to come. Vigilant yes, panicked, no.

* Note for non-US readers, I believe that .400 is a good batting average in a version of the game that we know as rounders.

Chapter 37
Quantitative Easing and index-linked gilts – a little less information

Jim Leaviss - Monday, March 23rd, 2009

Central bankers passionately love inflation-linked bonds. Firstly, they keep governments honest by discouraging them from generating inflation in order to reduce their debts, and secondly they provide real "put your money where your mouth is" information as to where the financial markets think inflation is heading. Unfortunately, the Bank of England's new QE regime makes the information derived from index-linked gilts useless – and in a perverse way too.

Just at the time when everybody is worrying that QE is the first step on the road to the issuance of Zimbabwe style One Hundred Trillion Dollar notes (I have one in front of me as I type, the watermark is a picture of a buffalo's backside), we've seen a collapse in the expected future level of inflation in the UK, according to the gilt market. In February, before the Bank's QE announcement, the 10 year breakeven inflation rate was just below 2.5%. It subsequently halved to 1.25%. In other words the bond market expected half the level of inflation over the next ten years than it had before the Bank turned on the printing presses. As I said, perverse.

The problem is that the Bank's QE programme only targets ordinary gilts (£75 billion of them). Index linked gilts are excluded (for liquidity reasons) and have therefore missed out on some of this big rally. Conventional gilt yields have therefore fallen further, and dragged down the breakeven inflation rate (the difference between nominal (conventional) and real (index linked) yields). This is probably an unintended consequence – but in so far as this "information" is used by wage setters and policy makers, might it in itself prove deflationary?

Since the height of the QE driven conventional market rally, linkers have caught up a little (the implied inflation rate has risen to 1.75%) – but the fact remains, if QE excludes linkers, then the information contained within their prices will become less valuable. Perhaps this is why the Bank has recently placed more emphasis on survey data (the Bank of England/GfK NOP Inflation Attitudes survey) when they talk about future inflation expectations?

Chapter 38
Equitisation of bank capital bonds

Ben Lord - Monday, March 30th, 2009

Over the past week or so we have seen an interesting development in bank bonds as around a dozen institutions across the UK and Europe have announced that they are tendering for their subordinated debt. Essentially this means they are offering to buy their bonds back from investors. Bank sub debt is usually issued with call dates (typically after 10 years) when the issuer can either repay the bonds, or extend their life and suffer an increase in the coupon rate. Banks have historically been expected to call their bonds at the first call date and there was a huge outcry in the market when Deutsche neglected to call a Lower Tier 2 bond back in December (as Jim documented here). The other extremely important feature of this type of debt is that the issuer can choose to skip coupon payments if they're not paying an equity dividend, and this does not count as a default as it would with any other type of bond. So, firstly, tendering for the bonds makes sense from the issuers' perspectives because it means they avoid having to decide whether to call the bond or to skip coupon payments. Although it might make sense from an economic perspective to not call the bond, and to skip interest payments, such action could potentially be very damaging to their reputation and ability to raise finance in the future. Secondly, tendering for the bonds also means they no longer have to pay out to service the debt. These two concerns are the main short-term drivers for wanting to buy back bonds with these options in them.

But what is really going on is this. Bank subordinated debt has been languishing for some time now. Banks can buy back 100p worth of their subordinated bonds at a premium to their current price to persuade investors to let them go, and yet generally only have to pay 40p to 50p in the pound (because they have been priced at 20p to 40p). And what this means in accounting terms is that, for example, cash has fallen by 40p for the bonds they buy back, and liabilities have fallen by 100p. The net result of this on capital is that the bank has a 60p 'gain', which goes straight into core equity, into the retained earnings account. And this is the highest quality form of capital. So investors make a small and quick profit, and the bank gets a very big boost to core capital. A further positive is that the banks can buy back Tier 1, Upper Tier 2 and Lower Tier 2, which are all different types of 'hybrid' capital, and get an accounting boost to core capital, which these days is the only type of capital that anyone cares about.

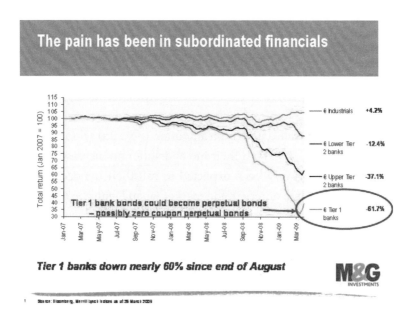

For the past few months there has been virtually no liquidity at all in subordinated debt. The only bonds changing hands were the cheapest, because for 10p you could buy 100p of bonds…it was basically option value. Now, though, there is at least some liquidity, and to that extent these buybacks are a positive for everyone. The news has led to a small rally in subordinated bank debt (see chart), but is not significant taken in the context of the past six months or so, during which period deeply subordinated debt has returned around -60%.

So at what prices are they offering to buy these bonds back? Well, prices vary from instrument to instrument but in all cases are significantly below par value, so those taking up the offer will be locking in substantial losses if they bought at anything other than distressed levels. By accepting 40p or 50p for their subordinated bank investments, investors are giving the banks equity (as explained above), and, although it may be happening in a different guise, this is a clear equitisation of bank capital securities, something that we recently argued was highly likely (as I wrote here). Investors seem to be willingly crystallising principal losses on their bank debt to exit the investments. From the banks' points of view, these exchanges are the direct equivalent of buying back subordinated bonds for 40p in cash, plus the remaining 60p in equity. But in these exchanges, investors don't even get the upside potential from the equity. Many have long been arguing Tier 1 is really worth 100p in the pound. We still don't think it is.

Chapter 39
What effect will the surge of government bond issuance have on government bond returns?

Mike Riddell - Thursday, April 23rd, 2009

This is a question that numerous clients and members of the press have asked us so I thought it would be worth writing a brief comment here.

Focusing on the UK, in yesterday's budget, chancellor Alistair Darling said that gross gilt issuance will be £220bn this financial year, which is easily a record. There is much speculation as to whether the market is able to digest this much issuance. If there is a lack of demand, or 'indigestion', then prices will have to fall and yields to rise until appetite for gilts returns.

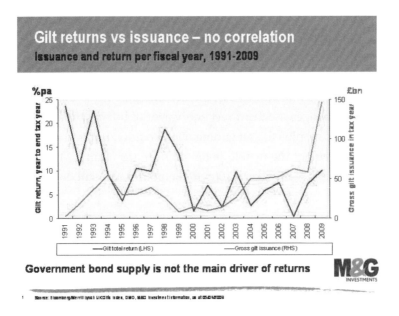

Gilt returns vs issuance – no correlation
Issuance and return per fiscal year, 1991-2009

Government bond supply is not the main driver of returns

The chart shows the relationship between gross gilt issuance in each fiscal year since 1991 against the total return from gilts in that period. There is no relationship. It's also a similar story if you measure gilt issuance as a percentage of GDP, or look at net gilt issuance rather than gross gilt issuance.

A lack of correlation is not to say that it doesn't matter if the supply of government bonds is huge – clearly it does matter. The law of economics says that if the supply of something increases, then all else being equal, the price will fall. But with regards to government bond issuance, all else does not remain equal. When governments issue lots of bonds, it generally means that the economy is in trouble. And if the economy is in trouble, it means that spare capacity is probably being created because unemployment is going up and wages are stagnant (or perhaps even falling). These things all put downward pressure on inflation. If inflation falls and interest rates are low or falling, then locking into a high fixed interest rate (at least 'high' relative to cash interest rates) is very attractive, and demand for government bonds increases. Yields therefore fall and prices rise. This is exactly what happened last year in the UK – 2008 was the biggest year for gilt issuance but was still a very good year for gilt returns.

What will cause demand for gilts to rise over the next year to equal or exceed the supply of gilts? It depends on what happens to inflation and economic growth. In terms of inflation, Alistair Darling projects CPI to fall to 1% this year, and RPI to fall to -3% in September before rising to zero next year. In terms of growth, he expects -3.5% for 2009, +1.25% for 2010 and 3.5% for 2011.

Slightly ironically, gilt investors should be hoping that the chancellor has overestimated his growth forecasts, even though this will inevitably result in the budget's numbers not adding up and even more gilts being issued than projected. Gilt investors should hope Alistair Darling is wrong because if the chancellor is correct about +3.5% growth in 2011, the economy will be booming at its strongest pace since 1999 and you can be pretty confident that government bond yields will be quite a bit higher.

Much can happen between now and 2011, and his growth projection is certainly possible, but at the moment our view is that it is unlikely that UK growth will be this strong. If UK economic growth does indeed fall short of his projections, then it's also likely that inflation will fall short too. And if your core scenario is that sterling won't collapse (which would put upwards pressure on inflation), then gilt yields are very capable of going lower.

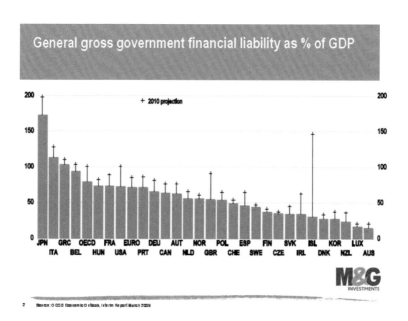

2   Source: OECD Economic Outlook, Interim Report March 2009

Finally, as we've mentioned previously on this blog, don't forget what happened to Japan. There are of course many differences between the UK and Japanese economies, but an important lesson is that large issuance doesn't mean government bond yields must rise. The OECD expects Japan's ratio of public debt to GDP to rise to 197% next year, more than two times as much as for France, Germany and the UK (see chart). Japanese government debt has tripled since 1996. And yet today, 10 year Japanese government bonds yield 1.4%, and got as low as 0.4% in 2003.

Chapter 40
Reaction to S&P putting UK sovereign debt on negative outlook

Mike Riddell - Thursday, May 21st, 2009

This morning S&P announced that the outlook on UK's long term sovereign credit rating was put on negative outlook. It's important to stress that a change in rating outlook does not mean that a downgrade to AA is inevitable, but obviously the risk has increased (S&P say the chance is "one in three"). The primary reason for the change was that the "UK's net general government debt may approach 100% of GDP and remain near that level in the medium term". 10 year gilt yields initially spiked 13 basis points on the news, but have since recovered most of the lost ground.

In truth it's a bit of a surprise that people were surprised. Firstly, it's been clear for some time that the UK's government debt is approaching 100% of GDP. Indeed the OECD were saying this back in March, as can be seen in the second chart in a recent comment on this blog (see this link http://bit.ly/ttuRRk).

Secondly, as we wrote in October last year and more recently this February, the credit derivatives market has long been saying that the risk of default on the UK is broadly in line with an AA rated sovereign rather than an AAA rated one. This chart (data as at the end of yesterday) shows the 5 year CDS on a range of European sovereigns, and as you can see the premium for insuring against the risk of default on Germany and France (both rated AAA) has been considerably lower than the premium for the UK for quite a while. Since the end of last year, the implied risk of default on the UK has been more in line with AA rated issuers such as Belgium, Portugal and Spain. (Note that if the credit derivative market is anything to go by, Switzerland and particularly Austria may soon find their AAA rating under threat too.)

So does it matter if the UK does eventually get downgraded to AA? Judging by this morning's very successful UK government bond issue, not much. The UK's Debt Management Office issued £5bn of UK gilts maturing in 2014, and the issue attracted bids for 2.6 times the amount offered. This was impressive considering that, as RBC have pointed out, it was the biggest ever nominal amount of bonds sold in a single operation. Also, a credit rating downgrade doesn't necessarily mean government bond yields will rise – Moody's downgraded Japan to A2 in June 2002, which was lower than the credit rating of Botswana at the time, and that didn't stop 10 year Japanese government bond yields getting to 0.4% in May 2003. And lastly, what do the credit rating agencies know anyway – as we've previously documented on this blog, Moody's rated Iceland AAA until May 2008.

Chapter 41
Bradford & Bingley skip bond coupons – is this legal?

Gordon Harding - Thursday, May 28th, 2009

We've had a question from a reader of this blog about yesterday's announcement that Bradford & Bingley will be skipping coupon payments on some of its bonds and whether this constitutes an event of default.

Actually it doesn't, and why not? Well, because HMT says so…

Back in February the government made changes to the terms of its nationalisation of B&B, using power it gave itself under the new Banking Act. HMT amended the Transfer Order through which B&B was nationalised to explicitly allow non-payment of coupons on B&B's Lower Tier 2 (LT2) dated subordinated debt, and to rank it pari passu with preference shares in liquidation.

This meant that from that day onwards B&B LT2 instruments had NO event of default (neither coupon non-payment nor non-repayment of principal count as events of default), making them effectively Upper Tier 2 (UT2) instruments in every way (it was always the case that banks could defer interest payments on UT2 debt in certain cases), except that they now expressly ranked pari passu with preference shares in liquidation.

B&B had already said it would only make payments until the end of May, and after that would submit a restructuring plan that was unlikely to see any payments being made to subordinated debt holders. So yesterday's announcement that it won't be paying coupons on three of its Tier 2 securities (one lower

T2 and two UT2 bonds with a nominal value of around £325m), which have coupon dates in July, came as no surprise.

The only continuing confusion is whether this triggers an event of default on subordinated bond Credit Default Swap (CDS) contracts, and if so, whether this credit event would also apply to the senior CDS as well. Trader speculation is rife, with varying interpretations, but no clarity yet from the trade body ISDA. The CDS market remains an immature one, and stressed events like this nationalisation show that participants need to be very cautious about the protections that they think they've bought or sold.

Chapter 42
Greece – the next country getting roughed up by the Bond Vigilantes

Mike Riddell - Thursday, November 19th, 2009

The original 'Bond Vigilantes' were the bond investors who reacted to authorities' loose monetary or fiscal policies by forcing sovereign bond yields higher, thus punishing central banks or governments by increasing the cost of issuing further debt. Right now, the Bond Vigilantes are hunting around the world like a pack of wolves. Japan was the prey a few weeks ago (see recent blog comment here), but the winds have changed slightly and the wolves have caught a new scent. As the chart shows, the credit derivative market is implying that the risk of a Greek default in the next five years is about the same as the risk of a Russian default, and Greece is now deemed a higher risk credit than the Philippines (BB-), Colombia (BB+) or Panama (BB+). In fact this data is as at yesterday's close, and Greek 5y CDS has today widened further to 182-87. At the beginning of November, 10 year Greek government bonds had an excess yield of 1.4% over German government bonds, and they now have an excess yield of over 1.7%.

Risk of Greece defaulting has steadily climbed
5 year CDS

Spread (bps)

Russia	**193**
Greece	**184**
Philippines	**178**
Colombia	**149**
Panama	**137**

Greece now trading like an emerging market country

M&G INVESTMENTS

¹ Source : Bloomberg, November 2009

It's been known for a while that Greece has structural fiscal problems and un-reliable statistics (in Trichet's own words, there is a "problem with credibility"). The main issue facing Greece, however, is that neither the Greek authorities nor the Greek population seem prepared to do much about it. A new Greek government was voted in after the previous government lost the election that it itself called in an effort to win a mandate for its proposed package. In January this year, the Greek deficit was projected to be – 3.7%, but it's been steadily revised upwards, to the point that the new government projects a 12.7% budget deficit for this year and 9.4% next year. The EC projects a more realistic deficit of 12.4% for 2010. (You may recall that a 3% budget deficit was originally an entry condition to join the Eurozone – it seems Greece has been fudging its budgets for a while.)

Things have all properly kicked off in the last week couple of weeks. The European Commission highlighted that there has been a "lack of effective action" in Greece in sorting out its public finances, a statement that was probably a reaction to the less than credible budget put forward by the new government (increases in health, education and welfare spending, with little in the way of tax rises and spending cuts). Then last week it was rumoured that the Bank of

Greece had advised Greek banks to sell part of their government bond holdings (officially denied), though it seems that they have asked Greek banks to be prudent and try to find alternative ways to fund themselves, as some of the extraordinary stimulus measures are being wound down. Investors are also concerned that Greek banks may find that Greek government bonds could become more expensive as collateral if further rating downgrades occur (the ECB has said that a haircut add-on will be applied to all assets rated below A-, which is where Greece is rated by Fitch and S&P, and Fitch has Greece on negative outlook). You can add into the mix the fact that the Greek economy is struggling versus its peers – unlike the Eurozone, which is out of recession, Greece is still in recession – and it becomes clear that the country is potentially facing a crisis.

If Greece doesn't come up with effective measures in the next month, it will be given notice to take measures to remedy the situation under the Excessive Deficit Procedure (Maastricht Treaty). If it continues to misbehave, then it may face sanctions and the EC may require a non-interest bearing deposit (I'm not sure how effective these measures would be – will it help Greece's problems if it starts getting fined as well?). Ultimately, though, it will be the bond vigilantes who move in for the kill, rather than the European authorities. This was echoed by the ECB's Gonazales-Paramo last week, when he said that the debt markets will punish countries which don't control fiscal deficits. And 'punish' is what the bond vigilantes are currently doing.

Chapter 43
Gilt supply update: back to a world of issuance exceeding buybacks

Gordon Harding - Tuesday, December 15th, 2009

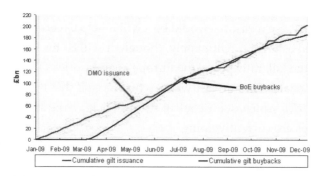

Which is more powerful? The exploding deficit or the Bank of England Quantitative Easing programme?

DMO has raised £203bn in gilt sales since start of 2009, BoE has bought back £186bn

In last week's Pre-Budget report, UK Chancellor Alistair Darling announced that gilt issuance for the current financial year would total £225.1bn – a shocking and record figure, although not far off the £220bn that was originally planned in this year's Budget. But while on one side we've had this huge volume of supply from the DMO, we've also had the unusual situation of the BoE busily mopping up gilts at a frantic pace. In fact as this chart shows, in Q2 and Q3 of this year, the BoE was actually buying gilts back faster than the DMO could issue them. This massive demand for gilts has kept a lid on gilt yields – 10 year gilt yields today are where they were at the beginning of June.

However, the demand/supply dynamic is changing and is set to change further. Looking at demand, the pace of buybacks has recently slowed considerably, as pointed out by Richard here. In November, the BoE 'only' increased the scale of QE by £25bn versus a £50bn increase previously, and year to date gilt issuance has once again overtaken the volume of BoE buybacks. In terms of supply, we still have around £50bn of mainly conventional gilt issuance to come over the remainder of this financial year, followed by another £174bn in the pipeline for 2010/11 and probably a similar amount the following year.

The quantitative easing pressure cooker has clearly kept gilt yields lower than they would have been in its absence, but the worry is what will happen once the lid is eventually taken off. Who's going to buy the gilts? Will the gilt market bubble over and make a big mess?

You shouldn't underestimate the power of the authorities to find new ways of generating domestic demand to keep sovereign debt yields suppressed, as the Japanese experience of the past decade has shown, and in the UK we'll see that a significant part of next year's gilt supply will find its way onto banks' balance sheets. But in our view there's a greater risk that gilt yields will rise from here rather than fall, and the prospect of a hung parliament and the potential for a UK credit rating downgrade increase the risks.

o o o o o

2010

Chapter 44
The big story for 2010: sovereign debt worries?

Jim Leaviss - Wednesday, January 6th, 2010

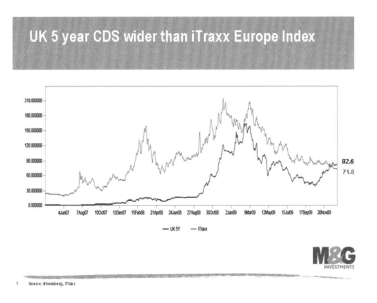

Source: Bloomberg, ITraxx

Happy New Year. Over the past couple of weeks, the cost of buying protection to insure against a default by the UK government has risen to exceed the cost of insuring a basket of European investment grade companies. The chart shows that 5 year Credit Default Swaps (CDS) for the UK sovereign are currently at 83bps per year, compared with 72 bps for the investment grade companies, which are all lower rated than Her Majesty's government and unlike the UK, the last time I looked weren't allowed to print bank notes to repay their debt. So it doesn't look right. But noises about a downgrade of the UK continue, and the plans from both the government and the opposition to reduce the debt remain unconvincing.

Elsewhere we've had sovereign debt scares in Dubai and in Greece, and yesterday in Iceland the President exceptionally overruled the legislature and stopped a payment to the UK and the Netherlands of £3.4 billion to cover money lost by savers in the Icelandic banks. Fitch downgraded Iceland to BB+ yesterday, although the bigger agencies still have the country in investment grade, but only just. Iceland CDS now trades at 470 bps. The decision by the Icelandic people isn't surprising, as the payment amounts to around £10,000 per person – a massive burden. I can't imagine that UK voters would agree to make such a payment to a foreign government should the table be turned, and the Icelandic economy is in a worse state than ours. This article in today's Irish Independent by David McWilliams is therefore a little worrying, as it probably does reflect the popular view that default is a better option that a strong credit rating or than having to wear a hair-shirt for a decade. Ireland has entered into significant austerity measures (including large pay cuts for civil servants) in order to restore the nation's finances. McWilliams concludes "Iceland proves there is an alternative – are any (Irish) politicians, from the President down, prepared to listen?". 2010 could be a year of angry populations and wobbly governments.

Chapter 45
UK money supply shrinks by most ever – QuitE a Dilemma

Ben Lord - Thursday, January 21st, 2010

Today we have seen the preliminary release of M4 money supply (so-called ' broad money'), and it could potentially be a very important piece of economic data. December saw a 1.1% drop in the money supply, the largest monthly fall since records began in 1982. Expectations were for a 1% increase. Year-on-year, expectations were for an 8.9% increase, but this came in at a meagre 6.4%. M4 money supply includes cash in circulation, retail deposits and wholesale deposits at banks and building societies and certificates of deposit.

M4 became a key piece of economic data post the economic crash, since it's a primary concern of monetary policy decision makers if the supply of money ceases and contracts. Trust and credit disintegrate, and monetary policy becomes utterly ineffective. Ultimately, this can lead to drastic deflation post a financial crash, which in a heavily indebted economy, can spell disaster (see this link http://bit.ly/u2sfMt for a blog from early 2008 on the importance of money supply). One of the key motivations behind the Bank of England's decision to implement exceptional monetary policy measures, and in particular Quantitative Easing, was to prevent such a collapse in the supply of money, and so to prevent serious disinflation or deflation. As Mervyn King said in his speech earlier this week, "the unprecedented actions of the Monetary Policy Committee to inject £200bn directly into the economy…have averted a potentially disasterous monetary squeeze" (to see this Bank of England link on the importance of money supply, please click here http://bit.ly/7moIAa .)

Mike wrote earlier this week about the rising inflation numbers in the UK. And whilst we feel that most of the cause of this spike was due to base effects, policymakers are likely to find it incredibly difficult to justify a further round of printing money through QE (as Anthony mentioned in this blog last month). Following the higher than expected inflation numbers, there is now a very strong consensus that there will be no QE extension next month, although there is a considerably weaker consensus around whether we could see more QE in the future.

The final M4 figure will be released on 1st February, when we'll get an idea of the breakdown and therefore why the M4 figure was so weak. In addition, it's worth highlighting that the Bank of England prefers to strip out the deposits of 'intermediate other financial corporations', which excludes things like counterparties and SPVs. Nevertheless, today's release is still alarming, because it suggests that QE's efficacy as a tool to increase the supply of money is perhaps not what we thought it was.

It is also potentially alarming that there is less money supply chasing the same number of goods and services, and yet inflation is still quickly rising. It's not our core view, but there's a risk that inflation could be more persistent than first thought, i.e. imagine what will happen to inflation if or when the money supply starts rising quickly again. This number will also be a concern to policy makers because it suggests an emergence of a monetary policy dilemma: the higher inflation number suggested that QE had served an important part of its purpose, the avoidance of deflation. But concomitantly, now, it appears that it has had less impact than expected on the supply of broad money – the money supply data would argue for an increase in monetary policy stimulus.

So which one of the two measures will policymakers give primacy to in February? Our belief is that the members of the MPC will still struggle to justify an increase in QE with inflation where it is now, but this M4 figure has just presented them with a much harder decision. Mervyn King also spoke of this lack of clarity in his speech:

"The headline in the Racing Post of 29 December said it all: "Quantitativeasing Maintains Perfect Record". Its Newbury correspondent reported that

"Quantitativeasing started as a red-hot favourite and had little trouble maintaining his unbeaten record. Ridden with plenty of confidence his task was made easier when Tail of the Bank came to grief at the second last. His trainer said 'I was delighted with the way he went through that testing ground'". Rather like the MPC, the owners of Quantitativeasing, winner of all three of his races in 2009, have yet to decide how many outings he will have in 2010. They are waiting for race conditions to become clearer."

We do appear to be living in a two-tier world. One part of this world (banks and investors) is awash with cash as a result of £200 billion of QE, and some of this cash for gilts is being invested in other, higher risk assets, which is bringing significant asset price appreciation and, perhaps, inflation. The other part of this world, the real economy, is in a very different position, and today's money supply data suggests that the cash that has been given to banks and investors is not permeating down into new loans and new credit to the real economy. Worryingly, at some point these two worlds will have to come back into line.

Chapter 46
Volcker Rules, OK for Bank Bondholders?

Jeff Spencer - Friday, January 22nd, 2010

Guest contributor – Jeff Spencer (Financial Institutions Credit Analyst, M&G Credit Analysis team)

In an attempt to reduce risk-taking at financial institutions, yesterday President Obama announced a proposal to bar banks from engaging in proprietary trading activity that was unrelated to customer business. He also advocated that banks be stopped from owning or investing in hedge funds or private equity funds. This address was met with concern from investors, with highly-rated government bonds benefiting from their safe haven status and global equities and commodities falling over the course of the trading day. Investors are wary about the potential implementation and impacts on the banks' profitability of the so-called "Volcker Rule" – named after the former Federal Reserve chairman who has advocated the move for months.

For me, it is important to delve deeper into President Obama's announcement. In the accompanying White House fact sheet, President Obama, echoing a small portion of the Group of Thirty document released on January 15, referred to "hedge funds, private equity funds and proprietary trading operations for [banks'] own profit", not "investment banks" or "investment banking" – an important distinction to bear in mind.

The equity market's panic reaction to the speech indicates that financial institution shareholders understand that trading activity has at least partially underwritten huge losses in consumer loan books in 2009, and may ultimately be more indicative of a fear that the days of banks' trading on the back of easy Fed money are numbered (shares of banks without sizeable trading operations were generally flat or up). Fed rules already prevent depository institutions from providing liquidity to non-bank entities within a group, but on September 23, 2008, the Fed allowed exemptions for banks to fund activities that are typically funded in the repo market. This exemption was extended on January 30, 2009 but expired on October 30, 2009. New limitations on the scope of trading by regulated banks appear intended to complement these regulations.

Credit investors may or may not have new worries as a result of whatever new rules ultimately come out of Congress, but it is fairly clear that there will be some confluence of 1) higher capital charges for trading/markets activities (neutral to positive for bank unsecured bondholders) and 2) more emphasis, for regulated entities, on lower-margin trading activities, as banks appear likely to be forced to demonstrate to regulators that any trading they are doing supports customers and is not "proprietary". We do not think at this point that this means that investment banking divisions of large US banks (or, for that matter, non-US banks that own significant US broker-dealers) will be forced to be spun off. It could, on the other hand, mean that non-bank financial institutions may have to close or sell their insured depository institutions. Whatever emerges in the financial sector reform legislation, it may not be the blunt instrument that the market evidently fears.

The limit on bank size is potentially the more problematic new rule to enforce, but only because it is so unclear how it will be determined that a bank is too big to fail, and what the consequences of this will be once it has been made. Again, the President's remarks need to be understood correctly: he said that he wanted to "prevent the further consolidation of our financial system", not that he wanted to break up existing banks. As with trading activities, existing rules already address this topic with a ceiling on nationwide deposits at one institution; the question is what additional measures any new limit will actually target.

These two prospective additions to the House bill (HR 4173, which has passed) and to whatever Senate bill emerges from the Banking Committee have not yet been outlined in anything like detail, so anyone who claims to know what their precise implications will be, probably doesn't.

Chapter 47
Exploding Myths

Richard Woolnough - Thursday, January 28th, 2010

According to many market commentators, the UK debt market is looking sick and is at a critical juncture. It is amongst the most unloved government markets in the developed world, which is understandable given the British inability to save in the boom times. Now there is justifiable scepticism that markets will not be able to absorb the forthcoming huge government debt issuance once the Bank of England stops providing life support to the gilt market when it ends the quantitative easing programme.

This consensus view is typified in PIMCO's monthly investment outlook in which the UK bond market is singled out as a market that must be avoided. In their opinion, the gilt market is resting on a bed of nitroglycerin. PIMCO point to the UK's relatively high level of government debt, potential for sterling to fall and domestic accounting standards that have driven real yields on long dated inflation linked bonds to exceptionally low levels.

We agree these are issues that face the UK economy and have commented on these points previously. However, like any consensus, it makes sense to investigate if this is correct, priced in, and when it might come to an end.

Firstly, the IMF forecasts that for 2009 the UK government will have a relatively large annual deficit of -11.5% of GDP, which is below that of the USA (-12.5%) but almost triple Germany's government deficit (-4.2%). However the

UK's total outstanding gross debt stands at 68.7% of GDP, which compares favourably with the USA (84.8%) and Germany (78.7%). The UK government has responded in aggressive Keynesian fashion to the downturn, if this medicine works then the action will be short term in its nature and will not leave the UK with a permanent debt burden, or the increase in debt could alternately be curtailed by the arrival of a more fiscally stringent government in this year's election. The UK has very little foreign debt and has been prudent by having the longest maturity debt profile in the G7. Outstanding debt and re-financing needs would therefore appear relatively manageable on an international basis. Not all outcomes will be bad.

Secondly, with regard to fears that our exchange rate could fall, the exchange rate has already collapsed by 22% on a trade weighted basis since 31 July 07. So a lot of the necessary adjustment has already taken place. This adjustment process is very beneficial for an open economy such as the UK, especially when many of our trading partners are locked into using the relatively strong Euro currency. By having a flexible currency and control over domestic interest rates, the UK is arguably in as good a position as anyone to grow our way out of our debt problem.

Finally, accounting standards have indeed distorted gilt yields as we have previously mentioned here. However, this accounting standard is designed to improve company accounts in terms of disclosing assets and liabilities of company pension schemes and this is surely a good accounting standard that should be adopted by many other regulators. The fact that better pension regulation in the UK results in lower long term rates makes long dated bonds – especially UK linkers – look dear internationally. But this dampening influence on gilt yields is a distortion that is likely to persist unless the regulation and the accounting oversight of this significant employee benefit are changed.

The view that the UK gilt market is one to avoid has some punch in the short term, but the consensus is exaggerating the risks the UK gilt market faces. Even if one agrees with the consensus, it is important to see if this view is priced into markets and when this will eventually come to an end. I agree with the direction of the consensus, absorbing that much new supply will be negative for gilts in the short term. However in the longer term the UK has the chance to adjust to the crisis through fiscal stimulus, financial reform and a falling exchange rate that might well provide the medicine required. The consensus that a bed of nitroglycerin is a dangerous place to rest like any consensus view should be challenged. Don't forget, a bed of nitroglycerin could be exactly what the sick UK economy needs as it is one of the oldest and most useful drugs for restoring patients with heart disease back to good health!

Chapter 48
What happened the last time the UK defaulted?

Jim Leaviss - Tuesday, February 2nd, 2010

Britain has run debt to income ratios way in excess of current levels at several points in its history. Around the times of the Napoleonic War, and both the First and Second World Wars the debt to income level exceeded 200% – levels that

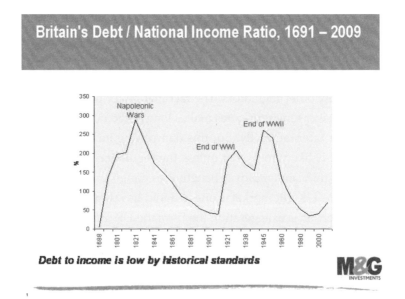

today would be regarded as crippling and would lead the markets to expect imminent default. Yet there has never been a formal default, and much was made about the UK paying off the last of 50 instalments of World War 2 debt to the US and Canada in 2006.

But it cannot be said to be true that the UK's credit record is unblemished. In their brilliant book, This Time Is Different (we've plugged it before), Reinhart and Rogoff do not have Britain in their very short list of six nations that have never defaulted (New Zealand, Australia, Thailand, Denmark, Canada and the USA). There are (at least?) two instances of the UK defaulting. In 1932, in the grip of the Great Depression, Britain (and France) defaulted on First World War debt to the United States – the so-called inter-allied debt. Britain had linked its ending of paying off these debts to the premature end of German reparation payments earlier in the year – academics therefore have termed this an "excusable default" where Germany was the real defaulter. The Americans didn't seem to be especially cross about it in any case, although it was done without consent.

Another event that I would classify as a default was the changing coupon on the gilt known as War Loan. Issued in 1917 ("If you cannot fight, you can help your country by investing all you can in 5 percent Exchequer bonds. Unlike the soldier, the investor runs no risk", the adverts said), the bond's coupon was reduced from 5% to 3.5% in 1932. You can read Chancellor Neville Chamberlain's speech announcing his plan in Hansard, here. This was a voluntary conversion – you could have had your money back – but the moral screws were on. Chamberlain ends his speech saying "For the response we must trust, and I am certain we shall not trust in vain, to the good sense and patriotism of the 3,000,000 holders to whom we shall appeal". 92% of holders accepted the new, lower coupon (probably not just for patriotic reasons, but because 3.5% was still a better rate of interest than was available elsewhere in those deflationary times). Today, we have seen the ratings agencies classify similar events as defaults, even if such disadvantageous changes were consensual.

Perhaps just as interesting is the question – why didn't the UK default more often? A paper called Sustainability of High Public Debt: What the Historical Record Shows by Albrecht Ritschl suggests that it isn't obvious why it didn't. Post WW1, growth was disappointing, in contrast with expectations of a peace dividend. Yet even during the deflationary years between the wars (1926 to 1933) the conservative establishment view was to run budget surpluses, and to go onto the Gold Standard (until 1931), which didn't allow a devaluation and thus help boost UK exports. Why the UK decided to beggar itself rather than default was in part due to the culture in the Treasury (the "treasury view" was hardline), and also due to the emergence of the United States as a rival economic power and financial centre. Post WW2, Ritschl argues that Marshall Aid was effectively a "rescue operation" that prevented a default. So reputation is extremely important in preventing default, the competitive threat from other financial centres matters, and having allies with deeppockets (Germany or the IMF in the case of Greece?) can also prevent defaults. Remember the golden rule – willingness to pay is as important as ability to pay. Britain was willing to accept austerity in the 1930s to maintain its reputation; Ecuador has defaulted with a debt to GDP ratio of under 20%.

So to the present day. This weekend the papers were full of headlines about Conservative leader David Cameron postponing austerity for the UK. Today, in what looks like a different view, his Shadow Chancellor George Osborne has committed his party to maintain the UK's AAA credit rating: "Judge us in the first few months of a Conservative government on whether we're able to protect our credit rating". I'd have thought that as a result, the UK's 5 year CDS spread would have narrowed a little, but it's stuck at 85 bps (we've written protection on Her Majesty's Government because although fiscally we face a crisis, we don't believe this will result in a default). Perhaps the market fears that the Conservatives are going to have a Devon Loch moment; the latest polls point to the forecast overall majority having slipped away, and a hung parliament is in prospect. With the UK economy at least growing again, albeit it only just, the chances of Osborne getting his chance to be Mr Austerity are slightly lower.

Chapter 49
What is the risk free rate anyway?

Jim Leaviss - Thursday, February 25th, 2010

The risk free rate is a concept beloved of micro-economists and bond math geeks. It's the building block of Modern Portfolio Theory and an input into option pricing models. It's supposed to represent the interest rate available in the market that is without credit risk and as such is the lowest interest rate in the market. The complete absence of risk has always been more observable in theory than in practice but in the last month or so, swap rates have fallen below gilt yields – can it be right that the lowest interest rate in the market is lower than the traditional risk free rate? Are government bonds still the right instrument with which to observe the risk free rate?

Interest rate swaps are a means of turning a floating rate cashflow into a fixed rate cashflow for a set period of time, or vice versa. If you decided to receive fixed rate payments for ten years, you would agree to pay Libor (reflecting the cost of short term money) and receive the fixed payment for the life of the contract from the bank with which you'd traded. Historically the fixed rate payment would be more than you could get by buying a gilt from Her Majesty's government. On average over the past decade it was around 0.5% more than the ten year gilt yield. This seems to make sense, as there is a risk that the bank counterparty that you have traded with disappears and can no longer service the contract, so the premium over gilts reflected credit risk.

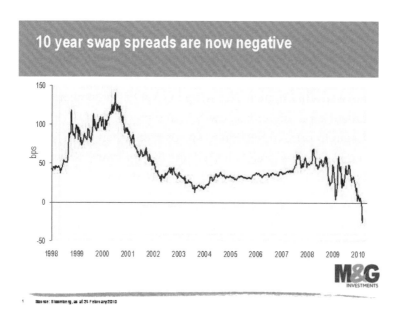

As this chart shows however, this swap spread (the difference between the swap rate and the gilt yield) has fallen substantially since the start of 2009, and in the first couple of months of this year it has turned negative. The ten year swap spread is now -0.18%. In other words you get a lower rate of interest in receiving a fixed payment from a bank than you would from a AAA rated (still!) government bond. Does this make sense? After all, if you are a UK investor that swap might well be with a government owned bank anyway, so isn't the credit risk the same? There are two reasons why you might want to receive fixed via an interest rate swap rather than buying a gilt. Firstly, if there was a UK sovereign default you would probably lose capital if you owned a physical gilt, whereas your downside in a swap default would be limited to having to replace the counterparty at a potentially less advantageous rate of interest. More significantly though, the markets are reflecting not just the increased risk of a UK default (which in our view is much less likely than is priced into the CDS market, at about 9% over the next 5 years) but more importantly the relative supply of swaps and government bonds. Gilt issuance will be running at around a £200 billion rate for the next couple of years, but without the market's biggest investor – the Bank of England has ended its Quantitative Easing programme (although not irrevocably).

So with an implied default rate of nearly 10%, the gilt market cannot seriously be regarded as "risk free" anymore, even if we do think that probability is nutty given the UK's access to the printing presses of mass destruction if we ever did get stuck for a few bob to repay our bond debts. But once the gilt supply glut is out of the way in a couple of years time (we hope), expect swap spreads to move steadily higher. The swap market has become an increasingly important yardstick for valuations however, and maybe the UK corporate bond market will begin to price in relation to swaps rather than gilts – the European corporate bond market has already been doing this for years, as has the UK population whenever we've considered a fixed rate mortgage.

Chapter 50
Could a Fiscal Policy Committee do for UK creditworthiness what the Monetary Policy Committee did to inflation expectations?

Jim Leaviss - Thursday, April 1st, 2010

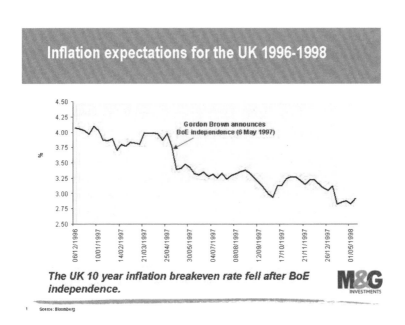

Inflation expectations for the UK 1996-1998

Gordon Brown announces BoE independence (6 May 1997)

The UK 10 year inflation breakeven rate fell after BoE independence.

M&G INVESTMENTS

1   Source: Bloomberg

The granting of independence to the Bank of England following Labour's victory in the 1997 UK General Election caused a collapse in inflation expectations. Whilst inflation expectations had been drifting down anyway, thanks mainly to globalisation and a demographic productivity boost, after independence was announced the 10 year breakeven inflation rate fell from 4% to 3.4% in just a couple of weeks. A year after independence, inflation expectations were down to 2.9%. See chart. With monetary policy out of the hands of politicians the long held view that the UK was a bit flakey on inflation faded away, and nominal bonds dramatically outperformed index-linked gilts.

Nowadays of course the UK has decent reserves of anti-inflation credibility (although funnily enough 30 year breakeven rates at 3.82% are nearly back at pre-independence levels), but we are definitely regarded as being a bit flakey on the fiscal side – just ask Bill Gross. At a gilt market lunch yesterday (hosted by BNP Paribas) former MPC member Tim Besley discussed his ideas for a fiscal policy committee (FPC) – "a politically neutral, expert body…that would assess the UK's fiscal position". As Besley's blog states, other countries with similar fiscal councils "have reinforced government's responsibility by raising the political costs of deviation". After a post-election kitchen sink audit of the UK's finances which finds that growth will be lower than forecast, off-balance sheet debt higher than declared and the cupboards bare, an incoming Conservative government can implement a VAT hike (which could take the annual RPI rate to 3.6% by the end of 2010) and buy fiscal credibility for the future by announcing the creation of a body like the FPC. Perhaps then we'd see a collapse in the UK's CDS spread from its current level of 77 bps to something similar to France or Sweden (46 bps and 35 bps respectively)?

Chapter 51
Lessons from Argentina

Stefan Isaacs - Friday, April 9th, 2010

The past couple of days have seen Greek debt take a bit of a battering. Spreads on Greek government bonds are the widest they have been since the inception of the Euro, and Greek 5yr CDS is wider by 100bps+ versus the beginning of the week. This seems to have been driven initially by nervousness around the anticipated bailout, with rumours that the Greeks are trying to renegotiate the deal that was announced on 26th March. More seriously though, Greek banks, who ironically were the ones responsible for buying a lot of recent sovereign issuance, have now asked for EUR14bn in loan guarantees from the government, perhaps due to recent numbers that showed as EUR10bn drop in deposits (4.5% of Greek GDP!). This could be the start of a bank run.

Looking to the relatively recent past one will find that Argentina underwent something similar. They went through their debt fuelled crisis in the '90's, with a bank run in 2001 as Argentines withdrew money from banks and converted into US dollars, culminating in sovereign default in late 2001.

The parallels between the two countries are quite striking. Argentina used to operate a currency peg to the US Dollar (abandoned in early 2002), effectively the same as having a common currency, in order to keep a lid on inflation. Argentina therefore imported US monetary policy, resulting in an artificially strong currency, and this resulted in artificially high imports (which meant a steady outflow of US dollars from the economy). The currency peg also gave the Argentinian public access to cheap US credit, which they were less than reluctant to use. Greece too has spent the past decade or so borrowing at artificially low rates of interest.

Corruption and tax evasion in both countries exacerbated their problems. Admittedly appointing political supporters to Argentina's Supreme Court and an (alleged) illegal arms deal could be seen as more morally questionable than cooking the books, but where markets are concerned dishonesty on any level is a serious offence.

The levels of debt of the two however are not comparable. Unfortunately for Greece, they are starting from a considerably worse position than the Argentinians. In 2001 Argentina's debt/GDP ratio and deficit as a percentage of GDP were 62% and 6.4% respectively. At the end of 2009, Greece's debt to GDP was 114% and the deficit 12.7%.

After the Argentinian crisis, the IMF, who repeatedly lent cash to Argentina in the 90's, produced an evaluation report entitled The IMF and Argentina 1991-2001. It's quite a hefty piece but on pages 6 and 7 there is a list of lessons learned and recommendations on how to avoid mistakes in the future. To me, the most interesting lessons are lesson 9 'Delaying the action required to resolve a crisis can significantly raise its eventual cost.....' and recommendation 4 'The IMF should refrain from entering or maintaining a program relationship with a member country when there is no immediate balance of payments need and there are serious political obstacles to needed policy adjustment or structural reform'. Recommendation 4 must be a particular worry to the Greeks. This crisis has been dragging on for a few months now without any decisive action having been taken and disagreements between Germany and the rest of the Eurozone over whether/how to lend a hand could be viewed as a 'serious political obstacle'. Clearly the disagreement is what has caused the delay in a resolution but the longer the policy makers procrastinate the more expensive an eventual bailout will get.

When Argentina defaulted, the government offered a debt swap valuing existing bonds at only 35% of face value, the worst recovery rate in sovereign debt history. 76% accepted these terms, but the rest didn't (and the holdouts are still fighting with the government today, which has locked Argentina out of international capital markets since it defaulted). With over half of outstanding Greek bonds still trading with a cash price in the 90s, if Greece does default (implied risk from CDS market is over 30% in the next five years) then investors potentially still stand to lose over half of their money.

A further worry is that when Argentina defaulted, the consensus (seemingly as now) seemed to be that there wouldn't be contagion. True, initial contagion at the end of 2001 was limited, but contagion increased through the second half of 2002. Only a $30bn IMF loan prevented a Brazilian default in 2002, and Uruguay experienced a banking crisis and defaulted in 2003. Argentina's default resulted in borrowing costs increasing significantly in the region, and growth for all countries stagnated. What is particularly worrying is that, unlike with Greece now, Lat Am banks didn't actually have that much exposure to their neighbour's debt.

Chapter 52
Swine Flu II

Mike Riddell - Tuesday, April 27th, 2010

Exactly one year ago, an outbreak of flu in Mexico led to fears of a global pandemic. 'Swine Flu' did indeed spread around the world, however for most countries it had only a limited effect on economic output.

We are now facing something that is likely to prove much more serious. This time the epidemic can be traced to Greece, and contagion is rapidly spreading among the PIGS. At the beginning of April, Portuguese 10 year sovereign debt

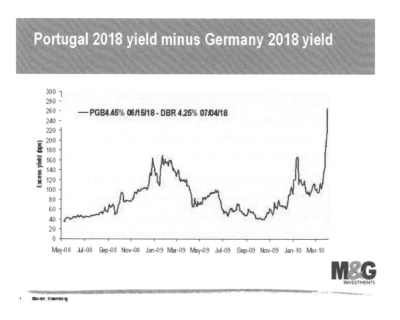

had an excess yield over German 10 year bunds of about 100 bps. Portugal began showing some worrying symptoms last week, but today things have got a whole lot worse. The attached chart shows the historical yield differential between a German and Portuguese sovereign bond maturing in 2018. The Portuguese bond was issued yielding 40 bps over the benchmark German bund, and today spreads over Germany have lurched to a sickening 260 basis points.

Who's likely to get infected next? The other PIGS look particularly vulnerable, and Ireland, Italy and Spain are all spluttering today to varying degrees. Ireland has been worst hit, with its 10 year sovereign debt widening 20 bps+ versus Germany, equivalent to about a 2% drop in the bonds' price. Italian 10y bonds are about 7bps wider, not helped by a weak auction earlier today, while Spanish 10 year debt is off about 5 bps.

But just as with the original swine flu, people may find that this disease can spread beyond the PIGS. Investors have (basically until today) seemed to consider EM sovereign debt to be immune, but Turkey 10y Euro denominated debt has sold off 7bps versus Germany (so it looks like birds can get it too). Meanwhile equity investors have seemed to be on another planet entirely, which may explain why the S&P 500 succeeded in closing at an 18 month high on Monday this week.

We've spent a lot of time debating what happens to credit markets if sovereigns continue to deteriorate. This is something we've been pondering for a while – see Stefan's thoughts here from February last year – but sovereign indebtedness has gone from being a small risk to something that's one of the very biggest risks, as the IMF recently highlighted. Can we have negative credit spreads, i.e. does a company like Telefonica potentially trade through Spain, or can GSK borrow at cheaper levels than the UK government?

We think this is certainly possible in stronger credits – in fact Johnson & Johnson short dated bonds already yield less than US Treasuries. But if the weaker sovereigns get into trouble, to what extent will, say, a high yield German cable company get affected if it only operates domestically...?

(Addendum: S&P has just downgraded Portugal two notches from A+ to A-, and Greece's long term sovereign credit rating has been downgraded three notches from BBB+ to BB+. It's all kicking off....)

Chapter 53
Alistair Darling – a Chancellor who will go down in history (in a good way); and was Margaret Thatcher really a public sector axewoman?

Jim Leaviss - Monday, June 7th, 2010

Now that the new UK government is bedding in and getting ready to unleash austerity upon us, I thought I'd quickly look back at the last Labour government and tell you something that you won't want to hear: the last Chancellor Alistair Darling did a very good job.

There were three significant tests given to him during his 3 year Chancellorship. Of those, I think that two were passed with flying colours, and on the final test we'll probably never know whether he was right or wrong. The first test was the run on Northern Rock in September 2007. This was the UK's first bank run in 150 years (since Overend Gurney crashed in the 1860s causing 300 companies to fail) – and at the time both the Bank of England, obsessed with the concept of moral hazard, and the Conservative party, would have let the bank fail. It's sobering to look back at how close we came to a full scale run on the UK's banking system at that time – and perhaps how close we would have come to civil meltdown had the ATMs stopped working. Alistair Darling's decision to support Northern Rock (and later the other major high street banks) was a game changer, and set a global precedent for the correct response to a run on a retail bank.

The second big game changer came a year later. US Treasury Secretary Hank Paulson was desperate to find a buyer for Lehman Brothers, the failing US investment bank. None of its US competitors would buy it without significant government support. In Andrew Sorkin's brilliant account of those times, Too Big To Fail (a must read) he recounts how Barclays were on the brink of buying Lehman – before a phone call from Alistair Darling made it clear that that would not be allowed to happen. Andrew Sorkin claims that a furious Paulson said that "the British have grin-f*cked us" – and Lehman filed for bankruptcy by the end of the weekend. We'll never know whether Barclays buying Lehman Brothers would have led to its downfall, and systemic implications for the UK banking system – but we do know that Barclays was subsequently able to buy the best bits of Lehmans out of bankruptcy for a song, without exposure to the toxic parts of the business. If the US government was the seller, yet no US bank was a buyer despite having had unprecedented access to the Lehman books, it should have raised a lot of warning flags. Again, a big call, and one that turned out to be the right one.

The final test was the decision to maintain fiscal stimulus for the UK throughout 2010, despite the widening budget deficits. Thanks to the General Election result we'll never know whether that would have been the right thing to do – certainly Keynesian economists like Paul Krugman are adamant that any contraction in government spending in the current fragile economic environment will be the trigger for a severe double-dip. David Cameron today announced "painful" cuts ahead that will affect "our whole way of life". So the jury is out on this final big decision – Darling's enemies will argue that the

Labour government of which he was a key player was responsible for the exploding deficit in the first place. Whilst he didn't become Chancellor until 2007 when things had started to go bad, the New Labour project did loosen fiscal policy when times were good (and befuddled current spending with "investment") giving deficits nowhere to go but up when the economy turned. Much of this current deficit problem was baked in the cake thanks to our deteriorating demographics, or results from the correct decision to bail out the banks – but Labour's pro-cyclical fiscal expansion must also take a share of the blame.

I wonder how we'll judge George Osborne's Chancellorship when it comes to an end? Whilst Nick Clegg has claimed there will be no return "to the savage cuts of the Thatcher years", it's interesting to note that apparently our "folk memory" of the Thatcher cuts is defective (according to a Stumbling and Mumbling blog post here). Apparently the Thatcher government only cut public spending in one year, and froze it in another. The blog's author Chris Dillow suggests that the reason we all imagine there was a huge spending contraction in that Conservative government is because public spending grew at a slower rate than under the previous Labour government. It's certainly interesting that the incoming Conservative government will be far more aggressive with the spending axe than Thatcher ever was – and perhaps Mervyn King's reported comments about the incoming government being out of power for a generation as a result of the austerity that they would implement isn't far from the truth. We'll find out in 5 years' time – if not sooner.

Chapter 54
China announces increased flexibility in its exchange rate

Anthony Doyle - Monday, June 21st, 2010

There was some big news over the weekend, with the People's Bank of China announcing that it was going to allow some flexibility in its exchange rate. The statement from the BoC points to the global economic recovery and domestic growth as the background to pursue further exchange rate flexibility. Markets have reacted positively to the announcement, with corporate bond indices opening up tighter this morning.

This signals the end of a de facto peg to the USD that started in mid-July 2008. From July 2005 to July 2008, the Chinese authorities very gradually allowed the Chinese renminbi (yuan) to appreciate by around 21% against the USD. Any appreciation of the yuan this time around is likely to be similar to the period between 2005-2008 i.e. modest and consistent. We should highlight that there is still some uncertainty around the timing, nature and potential scope of the new flexibility in the yuan at this early stage.

For us there are a number of main implications of this move worth highlighting.

Firstly, by keeping the yuan pegged to the dollar, Chinese exports are cheaper than they would be if the currency was allowed to float. There are many critics, particularly in the US, that believe China should be penalised for keeping its currency artificially weak. These penalties would likely take the form of trade protectionist measures. By allowing greater flexibility in its currency, the Chinese are reducing the likelihood that other countries start to introduce trade barriers in an effort to protect local industries. On this point, the timing of the announcement is interesting given there is a G-20 meeting this week.

Secondly, any move to see the yuan appreciate in value versus the USD is likely to be bearish for US treasuries at the margin resulting in higher yields. The exact nature of the impact on US treasuries is difficult to analyse. If the yuan appreciates in value then China will have less USD to invest into US treasuries, suggesting a weakening in demand. That said, given the appreciation in the yuan is likely to be measured it is unlikely that this is going to have a huge impact in the demand for US Treasuries in the short-term.

Thirdly, there will be upward pressure on global inflation rates if Chinese goods become more expensive due to the rising currency. Import prices for developed economies are likely to increase, suggesting higher producer and consumer prices. Analysing the allocation of items in the UK CPI basket for instance, we can see that many of the CPI divisions use Chinese goods as an input for the final product. This is similar for the inflation divisions in Europe and the US. Additionally, have a think about how many goods you own are manufactured in China. We can now see how a rise in the yuan can lead to higher costs for inputs which may lead to higher consumer prices. Given inflation is already above target in the UK this is something the Bank of England will have to keep a close eye on.

Fourthly, if the yuan appreciates versus other currencies, the purchasing power of Chinese businesses and households is going to improve. This could provide a boost to growth for countries that export goods to China and something that would be highly positive for global growth.

Ultimately, the announcement by the Chinese authorities is a positive step. A more flexible yuan will allow some correction of the imbalances that have developed in the global economy in recent decades. Given that China is such a large economy it is likely that the appreciation of the yuan will have many more impacts on global trade and finance than those listed above. We believe that any currency move will likely be gradual, thereby avoiding the large disruptions that a one-off revaluation would have on the global economic recovery. Watch this space.

Chapter 55
The European Central Bank withdraws the 12 month LTRO, just as banking system strains re-emerge

Stefan Isaacs - Wednesday, June 30th, 2010

A report in the FT today (may need free registration) highlights the lobbying of the ECB by Spanish banks to renew a one year funding facility known as the Long-Term Refinancing Operation (LTRO) that comes to an end this week. Banks borrowed €442bn from the ECB under the facility last year, at a time when borrowing in the market was either impossible or too expensive. When the facility closes, the banks that still need ECB funding will face two options – either roll into a 3 month facility, or into an even shorter 6 day facility. Banks worry that this shorter term facility will make their funding task more uncertain, and puts them subject to rollover risk when each facility matures.

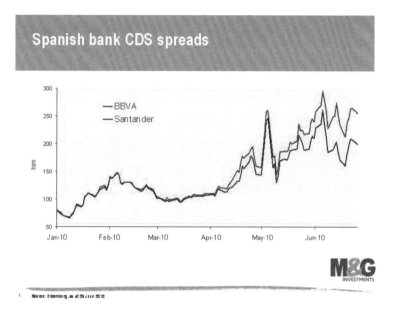

Spanish bank CDS spreads

Source: Bloomberg, as at 29 June 2010

This highlights two issues. The first is the difficulty that Spanish banks (amongst others) are currently facing in accessing the capital markets (see first chart). It will be very interesting to see just how much of the €442bn gets rolled because it will give us an indication of the reliance of European banks on the lender of last resort – on the FT blog they show the market's expectation of the roll, and the implications of this as an indicator of banking system health (the more that gets rolled, the more worried we need be). To what extent are banks able to fund themselves in the open market at all? This second chart shows that strains in the European interbank market have intensified in recent days, with 3 month money market rates up from around 0.65% at the start of May to 0.76% now.

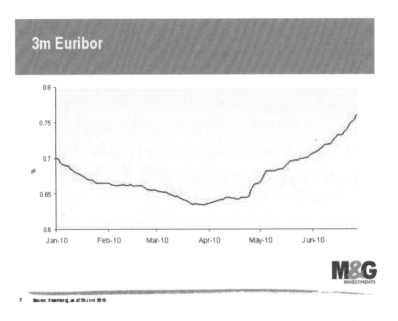

The second and perhaps larger issue is the risk to the anaemic European recovery that the ECB is taking. I've been critical of the ECB in the past, such as when it raised rates in summer 2008, and its obsession over fighting inflation. Now it wants to withdraw term financing from the market when arguably it is most needed. Shouldn't they be cutting rates? Where's the European inflation risk?

Whilst President Obama warns of the dangers of tightening fiscal policy too early in the recovery, Europe (and the UK) is backing austerity. The austerity measures that are being implemented across Europe may act as a drag on growth for some time to come. Who knows which is the right approach, but the tightening of liquidity by the ECB seems to be premature and misplaced. The European banking system remains on life support. Whilst European banks can continue to access 3 month unlimited tenders, the message from the ECB is that it is uncomfortable being the lender of last resort and that inflation remains the enemy. Unless the market's perception of the ECB changes I fear European banks will continue to struggle on their path to recapitalisation.

Chapter 56
Some thoughts from the Barclays Capital Inflation Conference

Jim Leaviss - Wednesday, June 30th, 2010

I went to the excellent Barclays Capital Inflation Conference a couple of weeks ago – although titled "inflation", a lot of the conference's content concerned the growing fears about the solvency of western governments. In particular, whilst the US Treasury market is currently seeing a massive flight-to-quality bid (10 year yields are now down below 3%) I came away worrying that it's difficult to see that the US has any plan to avoid medium term bankruptcy other than some hopeful reliance on the American Dream to magic it all better.

Ken Rogoff (Professor of Economics at Harvard, and co-author of This Time Is Different) accused the US Treasury of "playing the yield curve". With yield curves still extremely steep by historical standards, the authorities have skewed issuance to short maturities with the lowest interest rates (even though long dated maturity bonds would have historically low coupons despite the steep yield curve). Around half of all US debt will mature in the next three years – a tactic which keeps the US's interest payment burden down in the short term, but which is a "classic way" of triggering a financial crisis when rates start to rise. This is the shortest debt maturity profile for the US since the 1960s. A huge burden of debt refinancing, coupled with higher interest payments was the trigger for Greece's recent debt crisis. It's another reason why we disagreed with Bill Gross's "nitroglycerin" comments regarding the UK – the average maturity of the gilt market is around 14 years, compared with under 5 years for the US and 6 and 7 years for Germany and France. A "buyers' strike" should be a little less problematic for the UK than it would be for the other nations.

Rogoff also talked about the prospects for financial repression as a method for governments to create a buyer for their debt when the natural, economically motivated, buyer has disappeared. Financial repression is the process of making people own assets they don't want to hold – and the financial regulator is the important driver of this. In particular banks are encouraged (or forced) to hold more of their assets in less risky assets – i.e. government bonds – but also pension funds and individuals might find themselves being nudged into government bonds (in Japan individuals have most of their savings in the Japanese Post Office, which invests those savings in JGBs). Once domestic buyers are handcuffed, it becomes much easier to use inflation as a tool to reduce the real debt burden, especially in an economy like the US which has been steadily reducing the amount of inflation-linked debt it has outstanding as a percentage of the overall debt mix (although see comments below about the other inflation-linked government liabilities which stop inflation being the magic bullet policy tool).

Finally Rogoff said he'd be astounded if many Eastern European governments (and Greece) did not default, even with the IMF helping them. He pointed out that an IMF rescue package doesn't always mean an economy is saved; in fact in 1/3rd of the IMF programmes since the 1970s default has ensued (including Argentina, Indonesia, the Dominican Republic and Turkey).

If you were nervous about the US keeping its creditworthiness after Ken Rogoff, a speech by Ajay Rajadhyaksha (Barclays Capital's Head of US Fixed Income Research) piled on the anxiety. First the good news – the role of the US dollar as the primary reserve currency allows it to run excessive deficits far in excess of its economic rivals. Barclays have modelled the US's AAA credit rating with an overlay based on the percentage of the world's reserves kept in US dollars. On a stand alone basis, the US should have a AA credit rating, like Spain – but currently the US$ makes up 60% of global currency reserves, and this would allow them to run a 200% Debt/GDP ratio without losing their AAA rating, compared with the estimated 90% Debt/GDP level now. If the US$ became a bigger portion of global reserves (65%) then a 250% Debt/GDP ratio could be sustainable. Under current projections, only a fall in the dollar's share of reserves to 50% would trigger the downgrade to AA. Even with continued diversification away from the dollar by foreign investors, this looks a long way off. However, once it happens the acceleration is severe – when Japan lost its AAA rating the yen fell significantly as a percentage of foreign portfolios, perhaps helping to trigger Japan's further ratings downgrades.

That was pretty much it for the good news. Even at current low levels of interest rates, the US's debt servicing costs take a step upwards in coming years, as the Debt/GDP ratio rises to 95% by 2020. If yields were to rise by 2% across the yield curve the percentage of US government revenues spent on debt service would rise from a troubling 17% now to around 33%! And inflating away that debt burden doesn't work very well, as so much of the government's outlays are indexed to inflation (although I guess you can always do what George Osborne did in last week's UK Budget and change the inflation measure used to index benefits to one that is structurally lower, CPI rather than RPI). Rajadhyaksha was also nervous about the US government's contingent liabilities – losses on mortgages held by the GSEs (e.g. Freddie and Fannie) could be in the realms of $300 bn+. But the biggest contingent liabilities are the entitlements due to the US populations – and predominantly Medicare costs. After 2020, for every $2 trillion of taxes raised, spending will be $3.5 trillion. How do you close that gap without triggering a popular revolt, especially in an economy where median household incomes are only at the same level that they were back in 1998/99? Senator Judd Gregg, who some expect will run for the Republican Vice Presidential nomination next time round and sits on the Senate Budget Committee, suggested that the answer was to slash entitlements and cut taxes – this combination will encourage entrepreneurial spirits and reduce the deficit. It's one possible outcome I suppose. (Earlier Ken Rogoff suggested that the Federal tax take needs to go up by a massive 25% to put a dent in the deficit.)

A panel session with Adam Posen of the UK's MPC, and Former Fed Governor Larry Meyer asked whether Central Banks' independence is under threat from concepts like Quantitative Easing (buying government bonds as part of the monetary policy, but also incidently (?) keeping yields down at times of budgetary pressure – not unlike the trigger for the Weimar Germany inflation experience), and some increasing commentary about Central Bank inflation targets being too low (including from the IMF's research director Olivier Blanchard who thinks that 4% would be more like it). Posen believed that as long as a government is unable to fire the Central Bank Governor, and that the Bank is not made to buy government bonds in the primary market then independence is safe (although I didn't get why there should be a difference between the primary market and secondary market). Most importantly, independence is not about legislation, but about a "buy in" from society – for example, the Bank of England was able to be made independent in 1997 because it had gained anti-inflation credibility in the preceeding years, rather than prices subsequently falling because it was made independent. Meyer did, however, worry that the US Federal Reserve was more vulnerable to political interference than in the past – there was currently extraordinary hostility to the Fed from Congress as the result of the Fed's bailout of the banking sector, and its new lending powers. Furthermore as fiscal deficits become unsustainable, could the Fed really hike rates in a world where the US needs to roll over half its debt every three years without triggering a downgrade or default?

Now for a word on the inflation measures that we use. I've lost track of the times that people have told me that the RPI, CPI or some other measure systematically under-report inflation – or that these measures are useless for pensioners, who don't buy iPads, Blue-Ray discs and Superdry T-Shirts (sub-editors – please check that these things exist). Dean Maki (Barclays Chief US economist) and John Greenlees of the US Bureau of Labor Statistics put paid to a few of these inflation myths, and in particular pointed to the famous Boskin Commission Report of 1996 which concluded that in fact the US CPI measure was actually overstating inflation by something like 1.1% to 1.3%. The reasons why inflation measures tend to overstate actual inflation include substitution bias (the basket of goods doesn't change to reflect the fact that if the price of something rises, consumers will switch to a cheaper alternative), outlet substitution (not capturing the lower prices charged by a new Aldi store in the data for example), quality change (more reliable goods with higher specifications) and new product bias (price deflation is often seen in new technology for example, but it may take a while for that new technology to enter the inflation basket). Another big complaint people have about CPI measures is the treatment of housing, and especially the US concept of Owners' Equivalent Rent (OER), which is supposed to reflect the implicit costs of owner occupancy ("if someone were to rent your home today, how much do you think it would rent for monthly, unfurnished and without utilities?"). Recently OER has depressed inflation, causing critics to claim that this is somehow fiddling people with incomes linked to CPI. However, over the past 20 years or so, OER has actually boosted the CPI in most periods. The US does have an experimental measure of inflation supposed to better reflect the basket of goods for a pensioner (CPI-E), but it is only very marginally higher than the ordinary CPI. In fact there are no serious studies to show that western governments have suppressed the inflation measure to save money on inflation linked outlays (Argentina is a very different story however!) – the widely used inflation measures usually overstate inflation, which means both that inflation-linked bonds are good hedges for experienced inflation, and that there is a bias towards pensioners and other recipients of inflation-linked incomes being overcompensated.

If the CPI measure is so robust why does the Federal Reserve like to use the PCE deflator (personal consumption expenditures price index) as its preferred measure of inflation? Firstly it is chain-weighted, so it's more flexible in changing its composition weights to reflect cost-conscious goods substitutions, and secondly, unlike the CPI measure the PCE deflator can be revised historically along with the GDP numbers as fuller data is received. Because the CPI is used to calculate things like bond coupon payments, once released it never changes. The real cynic would additionally say that it is because the PCE deflator is usually lower than the CPI!

Finally, a senior sovereign analyst from one of the major ratings agencies was asked whether there has been any pressure on him from AAA sovereign issuers imploring him to leave their ratings unchanged. The terse reply was "There has been absolutely no pressure from the US or UK authorities". I wonder who has been calling?

Chapter 57
An update on the European bank stress tests

Tamara Burnell - Friday, July 30th, 2010

Guest contributor – Tamara Burnell (Head of Financial Institutions, M&G Credit Analysis team)

The publication of the Committee of European Banking Supervisors (CEBS) stress tests proved exactly the damp squib that most had been expecting. There was some additional useful disclosure on sovereign risk exposures (apart from a few German banks) but a decided lack of rigour in the regulatory approach. In total, only 7 "already failed" banks failed the tests. So all in all, the banking system passed the easy tests with flying colours, but at the same time is still on central bank life support and not strong enough to tolerate harsh regulatory proposals designed to prevent another crash. How does that work?

Indeed, since it was governments and regulators who were arguably being "tested" by the market, it is primarily the regulators who were the main "fail" candidates in this process. All they succeeded in doing was proving that the EU banking sector is too weak to be able to have a hope of meeting harsher Basel 3 capital and liquidity requirements by 2012. Stressing the banks to such a low hurdle (a 6% Tier 1 ratio after only relatively minor asset stresses) made it clear that regulators knew they were in no position to enforce Basel 3 on schedule. So it was unsurprising that the stress test results were followed almost immediately by an announcement from Basel that implementation of some of its key measures are being delayed until 2018, and that several measures were being significantly watered down (for a background on Basel 3, see Ben's video blog here http://bit.ly/vtyXn0). Indeed some cynics might argue that this was what CEBS had been trying to do all along, i.e. push Basel into changing its approach, to protect European narrow economic interests.

Banks (and regulators) seem to hope that by delaying regulatory reforms they will create positive sentiment around the banking sector. Indeed it has prompted something of a positive short term story in equity and credit markets, with banks seeing the opportunity to maintain their high leverage and asset liability mismatches for that much longer, and bearish investors have started to capitulate and accept that they can't maintain an underweight position in banks until 2018. However, this positive momentum is unlikely to be sustainable – the problems faced (namely overleveraged banks, sovereigns and economies, all with a huge refinancing hurdle to overcome in the next 3 years) have not been tackled, and the issues facing bank creditors remain unresolved.

The key question now is whether the political and institutional will is still strong enough to demand radical changes to the way banks operate, and, in particular, to the way that bank creditors are treated in times of crisis. Although cosmetically Basel has made some concessions to ensure that changes to capital and liquidity requirements don't precipitate the funding crisis they were designed to avert, behind the scenes some radical proposals are gathering steam. Regulators and politicians around the world continue to demand that next time around bondholders are the capital providers of last resort, rather than the taxpayer, and to this end regulators have been tasked with coming up with Resolution Regimes for global banks. As we see in corporate restructurings, debtholders usually have to recapitalise a company to maximise their recoveries – via a debt for equity swap or some sort of debt forgiveness – and a similar restructuring process is now being proposed for banks, so that existing creditors "bail-in" failed banks. This will require major legislative change and a change in mindset from market participants, so it can't happen quickly.

Ultimately these changes will lead to bond investors being far more careful about which banks they lend to and at what price, which could force a painful contraction in bank balance sheets. But we continue to believe that in the long-term the costs of not reforming the banking system and perpetuating the "too big to fail" assumption would be far greater (another crash) than the benefit of the status quo (high leverage, large asset liability mismatches, poor liquidity, high returns). So we still believe that important, painful and far-reaching reforms will be made, even if the global economy and banking system are not robust enough to tolerate these changes now.

Regulators are faced with only tough choices. Do they force through the big bang changes now, with the possibility that we re-enter a full-blown bank funding crisis? Or do they give the banks and their creditors more time to adjust to the coming changes? The latter would be done in the hope that by the next time we have a banking crisis we will have a system whereby even senior unsecured bank creditors could see principal write down or debt-for-equity swap features that help to recapitalise failing bank institutions when it is most needed (unlike the recent crash when there was no such support provided by debtholders of banks).

The banking regulatory and investment landscape is changing. And it is changing for the better: another crash will be less likely and the costs will be borne to a greater extent by all stakeholders, rather than just shareholders and taxpayers. It is just not changing quite yet.

Chapter 58
Turning Japanese I Think We're Turning Japanese I Really Think So (follow up)

Mike Riddell - Friday, August 6th, 2010

There is only one explanation for why 2 year US Treasury yields broke below 0.5% today (an all time low), or why 10 year government bond yields in Germany and the US are currently 2.5% and 2.9% respectively. Or, for that matter, why German 30 year bunds are now at just 3.2%. The bond markets clearly think there is a very real and increasing risk that the developed countries are going to end up looking like Japan. James Bullard of the Federal Reserve made this point in a recent academic paper, where he argued there's a possibility that "the US economy may become enmeshed in a Japanese-style, deflationary outcome within the next several years".

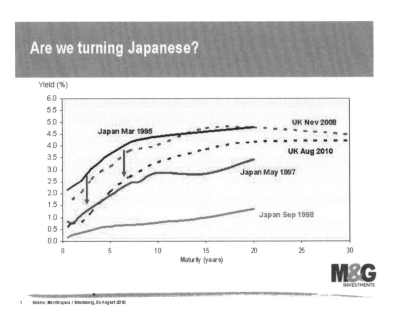

It's interesting to look back at how sovereign bond markets have moved since November 2008, when I last made the Japan comparison on this blog (see this link http://bit.ly/uzUPE5). In autumn 2008, the UK yield curve looked like Japan's did in March 1995. Just under two years later, and the UK curve and indeed many other countries' yield curves look similar to Japan's in May 1997 (see chart).

Is the market justified in believing that we're turning Japanese? Some may argue that the economic recovery in the developed world from early 2009 has looked distinctly un-Japanese. Preliminary figures for real UK GDP in Q2 were +1.1% (unannualised), the fastest pace of expansion since Q1 2001. US GDP hit an annualised rate of +5.0% in Q4 2009 and +3.7% in Q1 2010. While the recent estimate for US GDP in Q2 was a weaker +2.4%, global economic data (even in the US) is not (yet) suggesting anything worse than a modest slowdown.

However, Japan's growth initially followed a similar path in the mid 1990s – the year on year real growth rate remained positive in every quarter from Q2

1994 to Q3 1997, averaging a healthy +2.1%. The problem was that what appeared to be reasonable growth was a result of a huge surge in government spending and monetary stimulus. It wasn't sustainable. A lack of consumer demand, a broken banking system and falling asset prices then combined to feed into falling inflation. Core inflation (ex food and energy) fell from 2.3% at the end of 1992 down to 0.5% in 1995-1996. Headline inflation briefly dipped below zero in 1994-5, and both measures fell below zero in 1998 and have stayed there more or less ever since. The Japanese authorities weren't able to do much in reaction to this fall in inflation – monetary policy became ineffective once rates hit 0.5% in September 1995.

The worrying thing for the developed world is that cuts in the Bank rate tend to take 18 months to have a full effect on an economy, and it's perhaps no coincidence that the slowdown that hit the US a few months ago has come 18 months after the final Fed rate cut in December 2008. The only path left for central banks is unconventional monetary policy, and is something that developed economies began last year. While the policies haven't been totally ineffective (the Bank of England estimates gilt yields are 1% lower as a result) and we'll never know what would have happened without the extraordinary measures, money supply growth is still generally weak or falling. Developed world economies appear to have fallen into a liquidity trap, as argued by Paul Krugman here. This has serious consequences – if policy makers are running a Zero Interest Rate Policy (ZIRP) and inflation is falling, then real interest rates are rising. And if the economy falls into deflation, then you have positive real interest rates precisely when you don't want them, i.e. monetary policy is tightening.

The Japanese actually had a big advantage over us – thanks to Japan's huge domestic savings, the authorities were able to channel a huge amount of money into the domestic government bond market and were therefore able to maintain huge budget deficits and run up massive public debt levels (public/debt GDP is now over 200%). This fiscal stimulus is a luxury that most developed countries don't currently have. We've had unprecedented monetary and fiscal stimuli since Q4 2008, but bond markets are forcing most governments to withdraw fiscal stimuli. Further stimuli would increase the risk of sovereign insolvency.

So now, not only are we facing deleveraging in the household sector and the financial sector, but we're also about to face deleveraging from the public sector. The consequence of deleveraging ought to be lower growth and lower inflation and this appears to be happening. Monthly headline US CPI has now fallen for three consecutive months, which has only happened a handful of times since the data series began in 1947. Eurozone CPI is 1.4% year on year, and that's even before the fiscal austerity has really started. The UK appears to be the exception, although while inflation is a concern as mentioned previously here, inflationary pressure can be largely attributed to the combination of a VAT increase and the lagged effect of previous sterling weakness (and note that sterling has strengthened about 8% since the beginning of March on a trade weighted basis so currency strength should soon begin to have the opposite effect).

If you take the old rule of thumb that a 10 year government bond yield should equal the long term growth rate plus the long term inflation rate, then it's clear that bond markets are pricing in a grim scenario. Other risky assets arguably aren't though, and there's a clear disconnect. If the majority of the global economy does indeed go the way of Japan, I suspect that a lot of seemingly cheap assets will get even cheaper.

Chapter 59
Bernanke calls for a 4% inflation target

Jim Leaviss - Friday, August 13th, 2010

Well sort of. It hasn't got a lot of attention in the bond markets, but this week both Jon Hilsenrath in the WSJ, and subsequently Paul Krugman in the NYT have revisited Ben Bernanke's paper Japanese Monetary Policy: A Case in Self-Induced Paralysis. Bernanke wrote this in 1999 as an academic at Princeton University. In it he calls on the Bank of Japan to set a "fairly high" inflation target to show that it "is intent on moving safely away from a deflationary regime, but also that it intends to make up some of the "price-level gap" created by eight years of zero or negative inflation". Bernanke argues that an inflation target of 3-4%, to be maintained for a number of years, would give the private sector some confidence about the authorities' desire to get away from the deflation trap.

The BoJ obviously took no notice of Bernanke's paper, and over a decade on from its publication Japanese CPI is still very negative year-on-year. The question is whether Bernanke's plan to help Japan recover from the stagnation it suffered post the collapse of its commercial property bubble reflects his thinking on what the Fed should do to help America recover from the stagnation it's suffering post the collapse of its residential property bubble. Currently the Fed targets a long term inflation rate of just 2%, but also has an objective to maximise employment. We'd argue that the Fed has generally put the employment objective ahead of the inflation objective – its reaction function has always been to wait for the unemployment rate to start falling before it hikes rates (the lag between unemployment falling and the Fed hiking has been especially long in the last two economic recoveries – see chart).

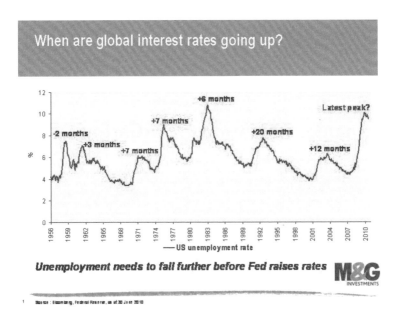

When are global interest rates going up?

Unemployment needs to fall further before Fed raises rates

However, a doubling of the US inflation target would cause carnage in the US Treasury bond market (who wants a 10 year bond yielding 2.7% when the Fed is targeting 4% inflation?) – and with one of the shortest debt maturity profiles of any developed economy, the interest burden cost of changing the target might be enough to trigger a credit rating downgrade (and in the medium term even a default?). For this reason alone I think that Bernanke is unlikely to talk about a change in the target publicly (although others, including IMF Chief Economist Olivier Blanchard have been arguing for such a change). Because of the political and public disregard for the runaway budget deficit, and the US Treasury's behaviour in borrowing short to finance it (50% of the US Treasury market matures in the next 3 years), Bernanke's hands might be tied. The positive impact on private sector behaviour comes from loudly signalling a change in inflation behaviour, but the reliance on overseas investors to finance the US deficit makes such signalling very expensive, and possibly lethal. So I don't expect a change in Bernanke's rhetoric around the inflation target. But actions speak louder than words, and we will see the zero interest rate policy continue for the foreseeable future, and continued excursions into the world of quantitative easing. As for the outcome of such policies, it would be foolish to put too much conviction as to whether the western economies end up looking more like Japan, or more like Zimbabwe.

Chapter 60
Why are TIPS yields negative?

Jim Leaviss - Monday, August 16th, 2010

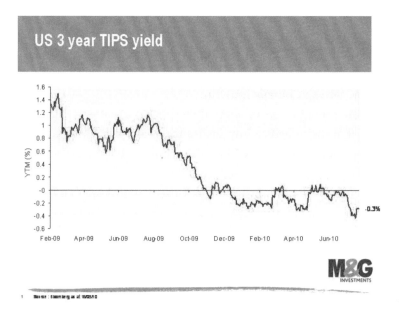

Last week a client asked us why US TIPS (inflation linked government bond) yields have been negative for much of this year (see chart), and we're not sure we gave a very good answer. This weekend, to distract myself from the monotony of doing laps of Richmond Park on my bike, I came up with these 7 reasons why an investor would lock in a return guaranteed to be lower than inflation over the maturity of the bond.

1) Unlike the UK index-linked market, US TIPS protect the investor from deflation as well as inflation. If over the lifetime of the bond you experience negative price inflation, the $100 you invested when the bond was issued is what you get back, rather than a lower amount representing the increased purchasing power of your dollars. So as deflation fears grow, the TIPS market has an em-

bedded option in it that turns your inflation linked bond into a nominal bond in a sustained deflationary environment – this is very much to your benefit, and is worth something. So the negative yield partly reflects the **option value of the deflation floor.**

2) Government bond yields traditionally reflect an amount related to nominal GDP growth in an economy. You have a choice – lend $100 to the government or invest it across the whole US economy and receive the average growth rate across all sectors, plus compensation for inflation. The efficient markets hypothesis says that ex-ante there shouldn't be a difference between the two, or capital will flow from one to the other to equalise the difference. If you buy an inflation linked bond, you can remove the inflation compensation element of this calculation, so the TIPS real yield equals expected US GDP growth over future years. The **market therefore believes that we are heading into a period of prolonged negative economic growth.**

3) The market might also, or alternatively, believe that we will get strong inflation, and that they **need to buy insurance at any cost**. After all, where else can you buy inflation insurance? Equities, nominal bonds, property and even commodities perform badly in high inflation environments. So there's a monopolistic seller of inflation insurance out there, and desperate buyers. When we buy house insurance we know we are overpaying relative to the risks of a fire or flood, but because the downside is so severe in the event of those things happening, we can't afford not to be insured. And at least there is competition amongst sellers in that insurance market. So expensive and incomplete inflation insurance is better than nothing.

4) As discussed in my earlier blog about the Barclays Inflation Conference, the official inflation measures probably overcompensate investors for their experienced inflation. The Boskin Report suggested this overcompensation could be as much as 1% per year for US investors. In other words a TIPS investor gets paid measured CPI, which is much higher than the actual inflation they experience – thus they can **buy TIPS at a negative yield and still get paid more than their own, actual, inflation rate**.

5) Another explanation for why short dated inflation linked bond yields are negative (not just in the US but in much of the world, e.g. France, Germany, Sweden, UK) is that the authorities' reaction to the financial crisis was to slash their central bank rate (a nominal rate), such that **negative real interest rates would encourage spending and borrowing**. Now, if you put your savings on cash deposit at a bank, the nominal interest rate is marginally positive, but the

real interest rate is sharply negative. If inflation linked bond real yields were positive in this environment then it would represent a 'free lunch'. So negative global linker yields demonstrate that markets believe that expansionary monetary policy will be run for some time (i.e. the central bank rate will remain below the inflation rate – US TIPS yields are only negative out to 2014 but positive thereafter).

6) The previous suggestions have been about the demand for TIPS, but we can also consider the supply of TIPS by the US Treasury. Whilst the UK's Debt Management Office targets around 20% of issuance into the index linked gilt market, the US Treasury has focused issuance on nominal bonds. So whilst the supply of TIPS has increased this year in absolute terms, as a percentage of issuance, supply has been in severe decline since 2006. Then it accounted for around a third of issuance, whereas by 2009 this had fallen to under 3%. There might be a **scarcity premium in the TIPS market**, which links back to the "buyers at any cost" argument.

7) Finally, one feature of a **speculative bubble** is that informed commentators can come up with six well thought out, rational, plausible reasons to explain an irrational price valuation. Perhaps this is one of those times.

Chapter 61
A letter from Ireland to M&G's Bond Vigilantes

Anthony Doyle - Friday, August 27th, 2010

Dear Bond Vigilantes,

The small nation of Ireland has received more than its fair share of press since the credit crunch started three years ago. The financial crisis has not been kind to the Irish economy, with the collapse of the Irish property bubble having a profound impact on citizen's net wealth and psyche. In fact, Ireland was the first country in the EU to officially enter recession. As recently as this week, Standard & Poor's downgraded Ireland's credit rating to AA-, its lowest since 1995. The "Celtic Tiger" was shot and wounded when Lehman Brothers collapsed.

I had previously worked in Dublin from 2007 until mid 2009 and saw the effects first hand that the recession was having. Union strikes, vacant shop fronts and alarming headlines in the newspapers were becoming an all too regular occurrence. On one occasion, an estimated 500 people queued for 15 jobs at Londis, a convenience store chain. The line of people stretched from St. Stephen's Green to halfway down Grafton Street. Things were truly dire, and an air of uncertainty was a constant presence in conversations with colleagues, friends and family.

With these memories fresh in my mind I headed back to Ireland with my brother and old man, with a view of sampling some of the Guinness and scenery. But first a bit of background.

The problems with the Irish economy are well known. So are the measures the Irish authorities have undertaken to consolidate the government's finances. Sizeable cuts to public sector pay and social welfare payments have helped to restore confidence amongst the global policy community and international financial markets. After a severe decline in growth in 2008 and 2009, the Irish economy has stabilised in 2010 and is now growing again.

But the path from crisis to stability and recovery is likely to be narrow and rocky. Ireland will likely rely on exports and tourism to lead the economic recovery. As Ireland is part of the European Economic and Monetary Union (EMU), they cannot rely on a depreciation of the euro in order to become internationally competitive. The Irish need to become more productive and have to reduce wage costs. Irish banks remain a source of uncertainty with higher than expected losses, uncertainties in global regulatory trends, and limited access to funding hurting the Irish financial system.

As we travelled around Ireland, speaking to the locals, drinking with the locals, having the craic with the locals, the state of the economy would often come up. In these chats, a few themes kept re-occurring. These themes were unemployment, emigration, house prices, and the banks.

The unemployment rate in Ireland deteriorated from 4.5% in 2007 to 13.0% in 2010. This large increase in unemployment reflects significant structural changes in the Irish economy. Unsurprisingly, the construction sector was a huge employer of people in Ireland and with the house price crash it is unlikely that these jobs will come back. Looking at the unemployment data in Ireland, it is a concern that labour participation has fallen among older males as they may find it increasingly difficult to find work in the future as the economy recovers.

Persistent unemployment is going to be a huge challenge for the Irish authorities.

For the first time in many years, Ireland is experiencing net outward migration. In this downturn, immigrants from Central and Eastern Europe have left Ireland in droves, whilst the Irish themselves have emigrated to places like Australia, Canada and the UK. Without emigration, the IMF estimates that the unemployment rate could have been as much as 2 percentage points higher. The concern is that Ireland is experiencing a "brain-drain" (present company excluded), and the Irish education system is effectively exporting a highly skilled and educated workforce (one that will pay taxes in their new place of residence).

Driving through the towns of Ireland we often encountered huge estates of houses that had been completed to varying degrees. These have been named "ghost estates" by the Irish. House prices shot up in Ireland during the boom years but were also accompanied by a construction boom, leading to a rapid increase in the supply of available housing (as seen in the accompanying chart), new shopping centres, business parks, and hotel developments. The dependence on the property market as a key driver of the economy and a vital source of tax revenue during the "Celtic Tiger" years has left the country with a set of serious problems that may take a generation or more to resolve. Certainly banks have tightened lending for new construction projects markedly, and it appears that there is little need for any new houses to be built in the immediate future. Some commentators have gone so far as to say the ghost estates need to be knocked down.

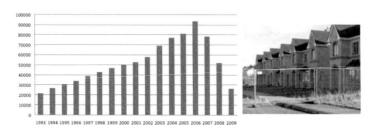

House completions in Ireland 1993-2009

No wonder the housing crash in Ireland has been so severe.

¹ Source: NIRSA, DEHLG, J uly 2010.

The National Asset Management Agency (NAMA) was a constant source of topic on the radio and in the Irish newspapers. The Irish government set up NAMA to transfer distressed property developments from the books of banks into a "bad bank". By February 2011, NAMA will hold €81 billion of toxic debt which is roughly equal to 50% of Ireland's GDP. The Irish have not bought into the idea of NAMA, with many suggesting that the losses incurred by the "cowboys" at the banks should not be offloaded onto the Irish taxpayer. Pure and simple NAMA is an experiment and only time will tell whether it was the right thing to do.

On the austerity measures that Ireland have introduced, I think a quote from The Daily Telegraph's Ambrose Evans-Pritchard sums up the views of the Irish pretty well:

"Dublin has played by the book. It has taken pre-emptive steps to please the markets and the EU. It has done an IMF job without the IMF. Indeed, it has gone further than the IMF would have dared to go. It has imposed draconian austerity measures. The solidarity of the country has been remarkable. There have been no riots, and no terrorist threats. Yet as of today it is paying 5.48% to borrow for ten years, or near 8% in real terms once deflation is factored in. This is crippling and puts the country on an unsustainable debt trajectory if it lasts for long. Yet Greece is able to borrow from the EU at 5% and from the IMF at a staggered rate far below."

It is particularly interesting if we think about the austerity measures that Ireland have had to implement and then try to determine what the possible impact that budget tightening might be on the UK and a major European country like Spain. Through assertive steps to tackle the budget problems head-on, Irish policymakers have gained significant credibility. But that is not enough. Retaining credibility will require strong commitment and active risk management. The markets view ambitious fiscal consolidation plans in Ireland, Spain and the UK as appropriate and these plans will demand years of tight budgetary control. If new governments are elected, will they continue to retain a tight control of government spending in the face of rising public discontent?

The return to a self-sustaining economic recovery, with lower levels of government expenditure, is going to take time in the respective economies. In the interim, unforeseen fiscal demands may occur and policymakers have limited bullets left in the fiscal gun. With limited fiscal resources, maintaining a steady policy course will be required to minimise risks and sustain market confidence. We saw that the market retained some confidence in Ireland during the Greek sovereign crisis in May, when CDS for other European peripheral nations widened relative to Ireland CDS.

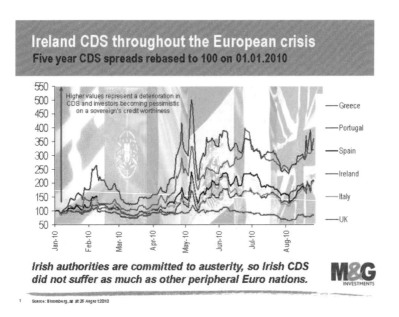

Ireland CDS throughout the European crisis
Five year CDS spreads rebased to 100 on 01.01.2010

Higher values represent a deterioration in CDS and investors becoming pessimistic on a sovereign's credit worthiness

— Greece
— Portugal
— Spain
— Ireland
— Italy
— UK

Irish authorities are committed to austerity, so Irish CDS did not suffer as much as other peripheral Euro nations.

Source: Bloomberg, as at 25 August 12010

More recently, CDS for European nations has been widening due to concerns about the ability of sovereigns to issue debt and a slowdown in the global economic recovery. CDS for the UK has been stable and confirms the market's view that the UK is relatively risk free.

The Irish have a tough task on their hands, no doubt about it. The restaurants and pubs are quieter than they used to be and the price of a pint of Guinness has come down a little (around €3.80 on average at the pubs I visited). In many ways, the Irish authorities have done everything that was required of them and this is pleasing some market participants. Mike Riddell bought some Irish 10 year government bonds on Wednesday after Ireland was downgraded, reflecting his view that the authorities remain committed to austerity and that the bonds are attractive at these valuations. Irish 10 year government bonds are currently yielding 5.60% compared to 2.16% for German 10 year bunds. The spread of Irish government bonds to German bunds is currently 3.44% which is a record level, so investors that are willing to take more risk are being compensated well to do so. Interestingly, the ECB waded into the market and bought some Irish 10 year bonds as well on Wednesday.

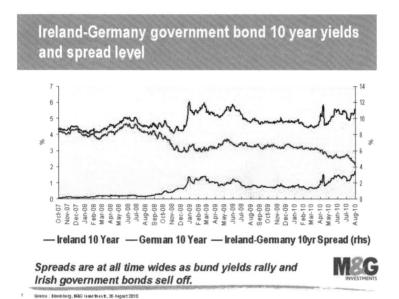

Ireland-Germany government bond 10 year yields and spread level

— Ireland 10 Year   — German 10 Year   — Ireland-Germany 10yr Spread (rhs)

Spreads are at all time wides as bund yields rally and Irish government bonds sell off.

M&G
INVESTMENTS

1   Source : Bloomberg, M&G Investment, 26 August 2010

There is also a lesson in Ireland's experience for emerging market nations, particularly in Central and Eastern Europe. In the 1980s Ireland was a relatively poor, peripheral nation on the edge of Europe with a weak economy. Foreign direct investment was mainly in low-skilled, branch plant manufacturing. The 1990s saw Ireland transform to high-skilled manufacturing and the development of a domestic consumer society. By 2003, the OECD estimated that Ireland had the 4th highest GDP per capita in the world on a purchasing power parity basis. Unit labour costs shot through the roof during this period, reducing Ireland's competitiveness in export markets and leading to inflation that was usually above the EMU average. The departure of Dell, a large manufacturing employer, from Limerick to Poland was a signal that Ireland had lost its edge in low-end manufacturing. It is important governments and policymakers in emerging nations learn from Ireland's mistakes.

Ireland will push through this crisis, but there are going to be some bumps along the way. And apart from analysing the state of the Irish economy in this letter, I'm also going to let you know what are "must-do's" if you visit Ireland. Stay in a fishing village called Kinsale in County Cork. The Dingle Peninsula,

Ring of Kerry and Aran Islands were also highlights on my week long journey. Have a few pints of Guinness. Don't have 10.

See you all soon,
    Doyley

Chapter 62
A Nobel aim – to find the right match and reduce the poison of long term unemployment

Filippo Fabbris - Tuesday, October 12th, 2010

Hi everyone, I'm the new guy onboard. I started at M&G last week but the rest of the team is already working really hard to find me a ridiculous nickname.

Yesterday morning, I saw a familiar face in the news. My macroeconomics professor at LSE, Christopher Pissarides, had just won the Nobel Prize in economic sciences (jointly with Dale Mortensen and Peter Diamond). On top of being an exceptional scholar, I have to say that he is also a very good teacher and a very humble and approachable person, sometimes laughing at his own basic arithmetic mistakes while lecturing.

The search and matching theory that the laureates developed models how we end up with outcomes where unemployement persists even though there are job seekers willing to work for a wage that employers are willing to pay.

This theory on the frictions in labour markets is of particular interest in today's economic environment. The post-recession unemployment rate in the US (9.6%) and the EU (10%) shows little sign of improvement and raises concerns about the speed of recovery. As Carmen and Vincent Reinhardt pointed out in their research looking at historical slowdowns, in the decade after an economic crisis in a developed country, growth remains lower and unemployement higher than its pre-crisis level. This implies that part of the cyclical components of the recession becomes structural.

The centre piece of the search and matching model, the matching function, intuitively suggests that if the duration of unemployment is large there will be more mismatching in the labour market:

$$M = m \cdot U^{n} \cdot V^{n-1}$$

Where M is the number of matches, U is the number of unemployed workers, V the number of vacancies and m and n are constants. Note that m has a negative relationship with the duration of unemployment (falling when the average duration of unemployment rises).

This leads us to think about the problem of the duration of unemployment, which has risen dramatically since the beginning of the crisis, from an average of 17.3 weeks in December 2007 to 41.7 weeks in September 2010.

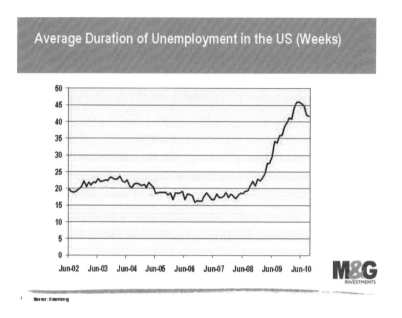

Average Duration of Unemployment in the US (Weeks)

The central message Pissarides shared with the world on the day he received the Noble prize is clear: "One of the key things we found is that it is important to make sure that people do not stay unemployed too long".

Long term unemployment is one of the major factors explaining the persistance in the unemployment rate as workers lose their skills and knowledge, and above all their motivation. Pissarides argues that government subsidies should be used to help companies to hire people back and benefits should be accompanied with conditions that encourage people to find a job much quicker. These policies may help to reduce the so called frictions. The Fed is aware that QE is too blunt an instrument to directly address current employment distortions – but with no political consensus for fiscal action, I fear that Pissarides's message will go unheard. In other developed economies, austerity measures are likely to include cuts in government subsidies rather than increases, which risks letting unemployment become entrenched.

Chapter 63
The currency vigilantes

Richard Woolnough - Thursday, October 14th, 2010

Last week we explored a topsy turvy world that quantitative easing (QE) could cause, with the lowest bond yields potentially occurring in the highest inflation economies. We noted that this would be the death of the bond vigilantes, as they are overwhelmed in their attempts to force higher bond yields by the ammunition of the printing press being put to work in government debt.

This begs the question – if the bond vigilantes are dead, who will take their place to enforce discipline?

The sequel to the bond vigilantes could well be the currency vigilantes. QE aims to produce a low interest rate environment with a traditional level of inflation by having negative real yields all the way along the yield curve. However, before you get there the currency vigilantes could well turn up to break up the QE plans. If the authorities are actually or are merely threatening to print money, then economic agents should act vigilantly and avoid this new money by exchanging it for other currencies or assets. It's the rational thing to do.

It appears that the currency vigilantes may have started already. Economic agents are dumping the QE currencies ahead of the switching on of the printing presses, and that can be seen by their desire for unprintable gold, commodities, domestic companies with foreign (non-QE currency) earnings, and currencies that do not have trigger happy central bankers poised by the printing presses. This has potentially important implications for asset prices, but also threatens a stable QE process. If there is a huge flight from a QE currency, domestic inflation could become rapidly explosive with no immediate growth benefit, so throwing up even more policy challenges.

The bond vigilantes could well be removed from the equation by QE. But in order to effectively implement QE – as desired by any member of the magnificent G7 who tries – this policy might well find its ability to enforce its domestic monetary policy destroyed by the currency vigilantes.

Chapter 64
An emerging market country issues lots of century bonds – reason to worry?

Mike Riddell - Friday, October 15th, 2010

Last week BBB rated Mexico issued a 100 year bond denominated in US dollars. It was originally supposed to be a $500m issue, but as is typical in any EM bond issue at the moment, the book soared to almost $3bn so the government decided to take advantage and make it a $1bn issue. It was issued at a price of 94.3, which meant it had a yield to maturity of 6.1%, or 2.35% more than a 30 year US Treasury. The bond's price has since soared, and is now at a price of 101 (yield of 5.7%, excess yield over 30 year US Treasuries of 1.8%).

A 'century bond' is a good headline grabber, and most people's instinct is to question why someone would want to lend money to a country whose credit rating is only 2 notches above junk status in the knowledge that you won't get your principal back until long after almost everyone currently on the planet is dead. However, once you look at the bond maths, it's not really all that incredible. The time value of money means that $100 in today's money is only worth $0.3 in 100 years (assuming an interest rate of 6% that's payable semi-annually). In other words, 99.7% of the cash flows from this Mexico bond will come from interest, rather than the final principal. The bond will actually behave very much like the 2040 Mexican bond that's been around since January 2008 – the 2040 bond has a duration of 14.8 years versus 18.1 years for the century bond, so there's little difference in risk. (As a comparison, the UK 1.25% 2055 Index-linked gilt has a duration of 35.1 years.)

So the existence of a 100 year senior bond isn't a worry per se - indeed, it makes sense for a borrower to take advantage of low US Treasury yields and (at least in EM) historically tight credit spreads to lengthen out its maturity profile. Such behaviour reduces short term funding pressures, and ultimately improves credit quality. And the existence of a very long maturity bond is hardly new; if you consider all the subordinated financial perpetual bonds that were issued in the noughties, we've seen far worse.

Century bonds – where are they now?

Issuer	Issued in	Issued at	Where is it now? (versus US 30yr Treasury)
Walt Disney	July 1993	UST 2023 + 95bps	UST 2040 + 159bps
Coca Cola	July 1993	UST 2023 + 80bps	UST 2040 + 152bps
Wisconsin Electric	Dec 1995	UST 2025 + 92bps	UST 2040 + 265bps
IBM	Dec 1996	UST 2026 + 80bps	UST 2040 + 178bps
JC Penney	Feb 1997	UST 2026 + 95bps	UST 2040 + 394bps
Norfolk Southern	May 1997	UST 2026 + 97bps	UST 2040 + 188bps
Ford	May 1997	UST 2026 + 85bps	UST 2040 + 410bps
Federal Express	July 1997	UST 2026 + 103bps	UST 2040 + 217bps
Burlington Northern Santa Fe	July 1997	UST 2026 + 85bps	UST 2040 + 163bps
Motorola	Dec 1997	UST 2027 + 65bps	UST 2040 + 342bps
Coca Cola	May 1998	UST 2027 + 105bps	UST 2040 + 190bps

[1] Source: Bloomberg, as at 13 October 2010. Pricing is indicative only

The worrying sign is simply that if a borrower thinks that it's a fantastic idea to do something relatively unusual because it believes that the terms to do so are very attractive, then it's unlikely to be such a great deal for the lender. This table shows what happened to the original century bonds that were issued by US corporates in the 1990s (see chart, and note that this is just a selection of the larger issues – century bond issuance peaked at 56 in 1996-97, with very few since).

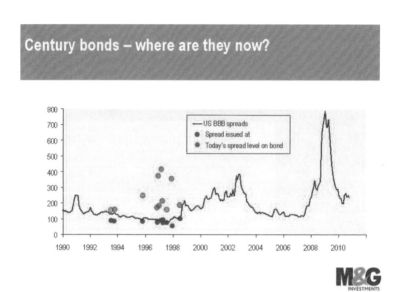

This chart is another way of demonstrating that the surge in century bond issuance in 1996-97 occurred at a time when credit spreads reached exceptionally tight levels, and credit spreads in all companies I've listed above are now wider (in line with the broader market), with some substantially wider. The red circles are the spreads at the time of each of the issues, and the pink circles show where the spreads on these bonds are currently.

Prior to last week, China and the Philippines were the only EM sovereigns to have issued century bonds. I wouldn't be surprised if Mexico's successful deal spurs a number of governments and companies into following Mexico's example. But if the experience of the mid 1990s is anything to go by, then let that be a warning – the Philippines' century bond was issued in June 1997, and July 1997 was not a nice time for Asian economies to put it mildly.

Chapter 65
See you on the other side

Stuart Liddle - Wednesday, October 20th, 2010

Now that the new budget has been announced by George Osborne and spending review disseminated, the coalition is lauding its merits and the opposition is deflecting responsibility for the deficit and exposing flaws in the cuts. Today's budget and public sector reforms will see billions cut from welfare spending, Whitehall budgets reduced, the retirement age raised, quangos culled and a permanent levy forced upon the banks. These austerity measures are taken with the intention of eliminating the structural deficit by 2015.

Many of these cuts implemented by the Chancellor were predicted / leaked and indeed austerity is believed to be the means to improving the UK's balance sheet after quantitative easing and a decade of high spending. Although the political parties will debate exactly who was responsible for the deficit and what the correct action should be, the consensus opinion is that cuts were required and indeed were the only suitable remedy to the situation in which we find ourselves.

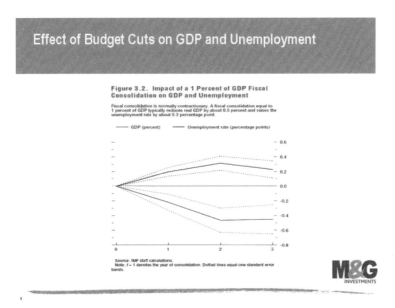

However a contrarian view is given by the IMF in their "World Economic Outlook" report they released this month. The data they have collated suggests that cuts do not necessarily lead to economic improvement, their data captured in this chart shows that a 1% fiscal cut in GDP typically reduces GDP by 0.5% and increases unemployment by 0.3% over 2 years. This would suggest the £81 billion (around 5.8% of GDP) of cuts announced today could lead to a 3% reduction in GDP and unemployment reaching 9% by 2012. It should be noted that the IMF's empirical data does not take into account any potential for further monetary stimulus (QE) and its beneficial effects. It does, however, provide food for thought and suggests that although cuts may be in the interest of the UK's long term balance sheet, they could have at least a short term negative impact on growth.

This is obviously going to mean that the UK economy is going to face a potentially dramatic onslaught of cutbacks reducing growth and increasing unemployment over the next year. George Osborne's message is that this short term pain is essential for the long term health of the UK economy. We look forward to seeing if this medicine works. As Ozzy Osbourne once sang – See You On The Other Side.

Chapter 66
How Senior Is Senior?

Matthew Russell - Thursday, November 11th, 2010

In the early 1930's Newfoundland – until that point a sovereign state – was struggling to repay its loans. Rather than default and face the wrath of the British gunboats, it was agreed that the country would be controlled directly from London. Fortunately things have moved on and debt now ranks below a nation's sovereignty in times of default. Banks are not so fortunate; they aren't protected from the wrath of their creditors.

Typically if a bank fails another bigger, stronger one is found to assume control. (Which, incidentally is what happened to Newfoundland after the Second World War – it was absorbed into Canada.) Bank failures are a messy business and regulators around the world have been trying to come up with new ways to stop banks from falling over and to limit the damage when they do.

Where senior debt will rank in future bank liquidations, and what the implications are for that market are some pretty serious questions thrown up by this process. Until recently it was assumed that holders of senior bank paper would be treated the same as bank depositors in a bank wind up, i.e. they would suffer no losses. Noises coming out of the western world's various regulators have pointed to senior debt becoming loss participating in future. I guess if you make a loan to a badly run bank, why should you expect all of your principal back when things go wrong?

Pension funds and insurance companies have thus far held a large number of these securities because of the perceived low risk of capital loss. If they still wish to maintain credit and duration exposure to the banks at the top of the capital structure they will be inclined to switch out of senior paper and into covered bonds.

Covered bonds are secured on a pool of mortgages. Therefore, if a bank fails, you should still receive your interest and principal payments, assuming the underlying mortgage holders continue to make the payments on their homes. In a fortunate coincidence, the new capital requirements that are being imposed on banks incentivises them to issue covered bonds as they require less capital to be held against them under Basel 3.

At the other end of the capital structure will sit contingent capital (CoCo) type notes, such as those issued at the end of 2009 and earlier this year by Lloyds and Rabobank. Regulators are very keen for banks to have this sort of counter-cyclical capital in their balance sheets. Once the capital position (currently the tier one ratio) of a bank hits a predetermined trigger level, these bonds convert into equity and therefore increase the portion of the capital structure that was designed to be loss absorbing all along.

The traditional subordinated notes in a bank's capital structure – Lower Tier 2, Upper Tier 2 and Tier 1 – according to some, will effectively cease to exist under the new regime. This implies a bank's capital structure will in future be made up of deposits, covered bonds, senior notes, CoCo's and equity.

Purely from a bond investor's perspective – setting equity and deposits to one side – it feels to me as though senior debt will become a rather esoteric asset class. Risk averse investors will buy the covered bonds that the banks are keen to issue, while those looking for higher yields will opt for CoCo's which they will be forced to issue. If you imagine a situation (shouldn't be too hard) where a bank gets into difficulty, its CoCo's are triggered but still falls into bankruptcy. The equity will be wiped out leaving a senior debt holder not only at the bottom of the pile in a liquidation, but also with a claim over fewer assets than they historically would have had, since most of the mortgages would have been pledged to the covered bond pools. Unless they invest in some gunboats, I can't help feeling that investors in senior bank debt might be in for a rather rough time in the years to come.

Chapter 67
US monetary policy – "drinking poison to quench a thirst" says the Chinese ratings agency

Matthew Russell - Monday, November 15th, 2010

"Drinking poison to quench a thirst" – that's Dagong Credit, the Chinese credit rating agency's, view of the Fed's monetary policy decisions of late. The recent money printing initiatives (QE2) and Dagong's perception that the US is less intent on repaying its debts were their motivation for downgrading the US from AA to A+ last week – somewhat below the AAA ratings that S&P and Moody's have for the US. Those US rating agencies rate Poland, Israel, Malaysia and South Korea in the A area.

Now presumably there is a fair amount of politics at work here, but nevertheless the report makes for an interesting read. It contains some of the most punchy language I've ever seen in a research report ("in essence the depreciation of the U.S. dollar adopted by the U.S. government indicates that its solvency is on the brink of collapse"). It's a good job that the report didn't move the market in any way, or there might have been a somewhat terse conversation with the Chinese government's reserves managers – who own a mere $868.4 bn worth of US Treasuries.

Chapter 68
How Secure is Secured? The new trend in HY issuance

Vladimir Jovkovic - Tuesday, November 16th, 2010

Guest contributor Vladimir Jovkovic, Credit Analyst

Issuance in the high yield bond market in Europe this year through October has already exceeded the total issuance for the full year in 2009. The novelty since the reopening of the market in 2009 has been the fact that high yield corporates have been looking to refinance senior secured bank loans into senior secured bonds, rather than the more common unsecured bonds. As such, the proportion of secured bonds issued by high yield companies after the financial crisis has been ~40% of total issuance compared with the more muted 10-15% level before the crisis (see chart).

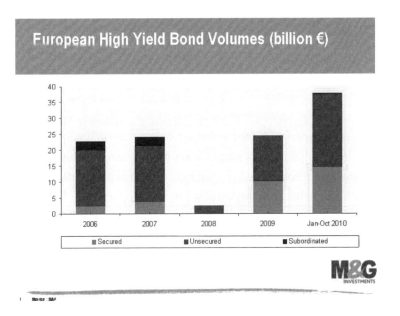

European High Yield Bond Volumes (billion €)

Part of the reason in the shift has been the recycling of loans associated with LBOs into the bond market as the primary loan market effectively shut down. As banks repair their balance sheets and restrict their lending, the public bond market is stepping in to fill the gap.

The question then arises, how will the relationship between senior secured bondholders and senior secured lenders develop? Will lenders continue to have disproportionate control on enforcement of security? Will senior secured bonds create more stability in the high yield market? The answers to these questions will no doubt emerge with time, but meanwhile and more fundamentally, how secure are secured bonds?

For a start, the 'Senior Secured' label is not a panacea for bullet proof security. Often the 'Secured' label is in fact misleading once you delve into the documentation. Secured bonds often involve pledging security on physical assets (for example plant and machinery), typically with a limit on the proportion of assets and cash flow derived from the assets covered. This in itself will partially define the security of the bond. However, some secured bonds have a security which consists of equity in subsidiaries of the issuer – for example Polish Television Holding which issued bonds secured by share pledges on its stake in TVN, a broadcaster. This is clearly not as secure as security against physical assets; and, therefore, the question then becomes whether these soft security 'secured' bonds are justified to have lower coupons compared with unsecured issues.

Then there is the more contentious issue of relative security in structures that contain secured bonds as well as loans. In the case where senior secured bonds partly refinance existing senior secured loans, whether the new senior secured bonds rank pari passu (equally) with the existing secured loans will depend on whether they share the same position in the capital structure and the extent to which the security package shared is the same. It appears that in recent transactions when existing bank debt is partially refinanced with senior secured bonds the loan holders retain control, whilst when both bonds and loans are refinanced together bondholders have an opportunity to share control.

It is also important to consider the inter-creditor deed, which may determine the loss sharing arrangement between creditors and their effective relative ranking on enforcement. The inter-creditor deed has not always been made available to bondholders, which has made it difficult to ascertain bondholders' precise rights in an enforcement scenario. For example, the inter-creditor could specify that senior secured bond holders are not part of the instructing group for enforcement proceedings, leaving them in a passive position with respect to controlling negotiations, were a default to happen.

With the rise in issuance of senior secured bonds and their greater enforcement rights compared to the more traditional unsecured bonds, making the inter-creditor available to high yield bonds holders makes sense. It appears, at least for now, with recent high yield issuers such as Exova (testing and advisory services), R&R (ice cream) and Polypipe (pipes for construction) that the tide is shifting in favour of higher disclosure. Greater transparency in the market will carry the benefits of improved liquidity and depth of market as bond holders become better equipped to answer the question 'How secure is secured?'.

Chapter 69
Here's why Spain's in trouble

Mike Riddell - Thursday, December 23rd, 2010

The convention in the market is to estimate a country's degree of distress by looking at the yield spread over a 'risk free' rate. So in the case of eurozone countries, people tend to look at the spread over German government bonds.

While this spread is clearly important, it's more relevant to look at the absolute yield level if you're trying to figure out whether a country's debt is sustainable. After all, if German government bonds yield 1% and the spread is 3%, the country can borrow at 4%. But if German government bonds yield 4% and the spread is 3%, then borrowing costs are 7%. That's a whole new ball game.

The problem that the Eurozone faces right now is that not only have peripheral spreads been rising, but the risk free rate has increased too. German 10 year government bond yields have jumped from 2.1% at the end of August to 3% now, which is probably due to a combination of stronger European economic data, a sell off in US Treasuries, and the potential for a peripheral bailout to be very expensive for core Europe (Germany and France are hardly debt free, with public debt/GDP ratios likely to exceed 75% in Germany and approach 90% in France next year even in the absence of bailouts).

Long dated Spanish goverment bond yields are now at the highest for a decade, and this is a major problem if you consider the mathematics of government debt ratios. A country's government debt/GDP ratio is a function of three things: the change in a country's fiscal balance as a % of GDP, the difference between debt interest costs and nominal growth as a % of GDP, and changes in the stockflow adjustment (which tends to be relatively small). So assuming that a country runs a balanced budget and the stockflow adjustment is zero, if a country's interest costs on its debt exceed its nominal GDP growth then its debt/GDP ratio will steadily creep up.

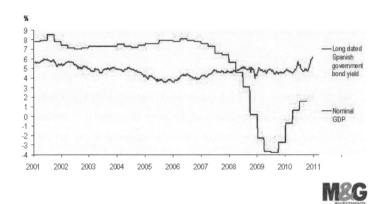

The average interest cost on all outstanding Spanish debt is currently just under 4%, which isn't too alarming. The problem is that long dated Spanish government bonds now yield over 6%. As the chart shows, a 6% interest rate on long term debt was fine a decade ago, when nominal Spanish GDP was running at 7-8% per annum. But Spain's interest costs will steadily climb higher as it comes to the market to borrow more money and roll over its existing debt. Any increase in interest rates from the ECB will accelerate the increase in interest costs and put even more pressure on the weaker Eurozone countries since short term borrowing costs will jump in tandem (five year Spanish government bonds already yield more than 4%). Spain needs to offset this steady rise in debt service costs with a budget surplus, which is not likely for the foreseeable future, or hope that its nominal growth rate jumps back above its borrowing costs, which is also not likely for the foreseeable future. Long term borrowing costs of 6% are not sustainable.

o o o o o

2011

Chapter 70
Titanic Issuance: Is This The Year Of The Covered Bond?

Matthew Russell - Thursday, January 6th, 2011

We have been musing for a while now the impact of new financial regulations on bank funding and how banks will structure their balance sheets going forward. I speculated a couple of months ago that banks would likely begin to fund themselves by issuing a combination of covered bonds and contingent capital. My sense is that the demand for contingent convertible capital in the market is currently pretty weak, which if I am to be believed, leaves covered bonds as the only option for bank funding.

Yesterday I think we got a glimpse into the future. Several European banks came to the market with covered bonds. Already this year (week) we have had €14.25bn worth of supply, and when you consider that the euro covered bond market usually issues around €150bn of paper a year, it does seem as though it's a level that may be worthy of some note. Even with about 10% of the normal yearly supply already done, sentiment is that there is a lot more still to come.

It has generally been larger banks that have come to market and such is the desire to issue paper, they seem willing to pay up. Santander, for example launched a 5yr cedulas (Spanish for covered bond) which priced at swaps+225 yesterday. A record wide level.

A preponderance of covered bonds is clearly not good news for senior debt holders, because in the event of a bank liquidation you are further away from the top of the capital structure and therefore have a claim over fewer assets than you would have traditionally had. It will be interesting to see how the covered bond market develops and what happens to spreads – what will dominate? Demand or supply?

This Titanic issuance of covered bonds is more than moving the proverbial deck chairs around to fund the banks. In fact senior and subordinated bond holders are being rearranged further from the safety of government and legal lifeboats.

Chapter 71
Emerging market inflation – a big risk to global growth

Mike Riddell - Monday, January 17th, 2011

The reasons behind the ugly scenes in Tunisia are down to a combination of political and economic factors, but at least part of the discontent stems from rising food and energy prices. Public unrest in Tunisia has spread to Jordan, where thousands were protesting against the government over the weekend, and demonstrations are also spreading to Egypt (10 year US$ bonds are down 4% today, and the 30 years US$ bonds down as much as 8%).

The problem these countries face is that food and energy prices are a much bigger percentage of an emerging consumer's shopping basket than for a developed consumer's basket. Food and energy therefore carry a much higher weight in domestic consumer price indices within emerging markets, which is something I discussed last year when going over some of the risks to the emerging market story (see this link http://bit.ly/rtgJFd).

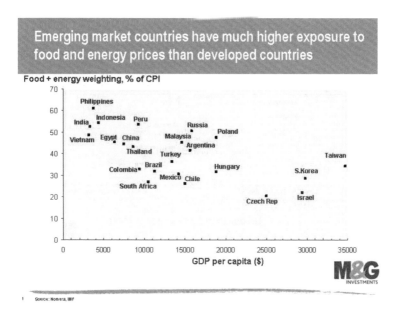

As this chart demonstrates, there's a reasonable correlation between a country's wealth (as measured by GDP per capita) and the weighting of food and energy in the country's CPI basket. Poorer countries therefore tend to be those that are most vulnerable to rising commodity prices, so of the major emerging markets I've looked at, food and energy constitutes over 60% of the Philippines' consumer basket, while South Korea, Taiwan and Israel's inflation indices have a far lower exposure. (Note that the latter countries should probably be considered 'emerged' rather than 'emerging' – Taiwan in fact had a higher GDP per capita than France and Japan last year.)

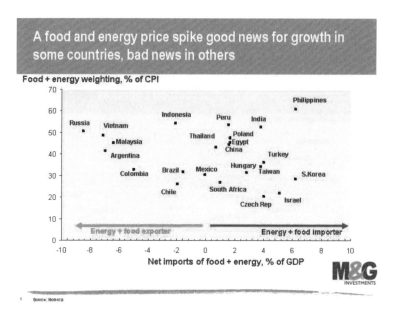

While GDP per capita is a good indicator of the degree that a country's inflation rate is vulnerable to rising food and energy prices, some emerging market countries would likely welcome higher prices if they're producers of the stuff. This chart from Nomura plots the weighting of the food and energy component in the CPI basket for a range of emerging market countries versus the degree to which the country is an importer or exporter of food and energy, where countries to the right are net importers and countries to the left net exporters. The country that would most likely welcome higher commodity prices is unsurprisingly Russia, while the country that is most exposed is, again, the Philippines, which happens to be the world's biggest rice importer.

The global growth drivers India and China also flash up as being vulnerable to rising food and energy prices. In India, the inflation rate was 8.4% year on year in December, driven by food prices climbing at 16.9% and today governor Duvvuri Subbarao warned about surging inflation, suggesting further interest rate hikes. China's official inflation rate is 5.1% year on year, and has only been higher in the last decade from mid 2007 to mid 2008. I wouldn't be surprised if China's unofficial inflation rate was higher still, and the authorities have responded by tightening monetary policy and allowing a degree of currency appreciation, both of which should result in weaker Chinese growth.

To an extent, higher food and energy prices are a result of expansionary economic policy in the US combined with a reluctance of emerging market countries (particularly China) to allow their currencies to appreciate versus the US dollar. Would it not be ironic if the very policies that US authorities have pursued to return the US economy to growth then proceed to be the cause of global economic weakness?

Chapter 72
Inflation Hedging for Long-Term Investors – the most important academic paper you will read this year

Anthony Doyle - Tuesday, February 1st, 2011

You would have to be living under a rock to not notice the increasing number of articles dedicated to the topic of inflation. The increase in inflationary articles has almost been as dramatic as the increase in inflation itself. Even 3 out of our last 4 blogs have been on inflation. Unsurprising really, seeing as we are bond investors. Looking elsewhere, the pundits have decided to focus on the idea of how an investor can protect a portfolio of assets from inflation. Having done a lot of research on the topic here on the M&G bond team, we would like to draw your attention to an IMF working paper entitled "Inflation Hedging for Long-Term Investors" which adds an interesting angle on the debate.

Alexander Attie and Shaun Roache tackled the subject of inflation hedging front-on, and discovered some surprising results in the process. Attie and Roache had a look at the asset classes that typically make up the core of long-term investor portfolios – cash, bonds, equities, property and commodities – and measured the sensitivity of asset class returns to inflation over a one-year horizon.

The authors found that "the ability of cash to hedge against inflation is heavily influenced by the prevailing monetary policy regime". This is unsurprising given the success central banks have had in anchoring inflationary expectations since the 1980s. It tends to be the case that when inflationary pressures increase, the central bank will act by hiking up interest rates.

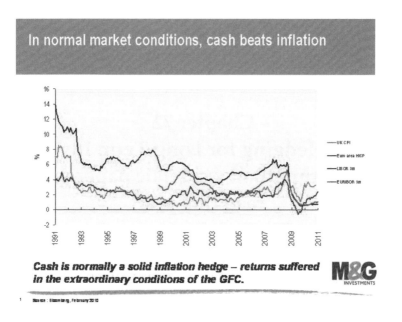

In normal market conditions, cash beats inflation

Cash is normally a solid inflation hedge – returns suffered in the extraordinary conditions of the GFC.

The most recent experience suggests that banks have been more willing than usual to keep rates on hold despite a pick-up in inflation. In the attached chart, we can see that inflation both in the UK and Europe has been running at a level that is higher than short term cash rates as measured by LIBOR and EURIBOR. This would indicate that whilst cash has traditionally been a partial hedge, since the financial crisis this has not been the case.

Both bonds and equities underperform if inflation increases. Looking at the analysis of returns since 1973, for a 1 percentage point increase in inflation over 12 months, the nominal annual return on a US Treasury bond benchmark fell by -1.33%. US corporate bonds fell by -1.91%. Equities experience even larger losses, with the same 1 percentage point increase in inflation leading to a fall in returns of the S&P 500 Index of -2.59%. Property, as measured by the FTSE NAREIT index does even worse, with returns falling by -3.48%.

Many investors point to the fact that commercial property rent reviews may be indexed to an inflationary measure, like RPI in the UK or HICP in Europe. However, because owners of property have generally levered their deposit through a loan, the cost of financing that loan will rise if interest rates increase to combat rising inflation. Pricing pressures on property arise when financing costs increase to material levels, causing both retail and commercial property prices to fall.

Commodities, as measured by the CRB Index, provide an effective hedge under this analysis with a 1 percentage point increase in the US CPI resulting in an increase of 3.77%. The gold spot price does particularly well, with the price increasing by 6.87%.

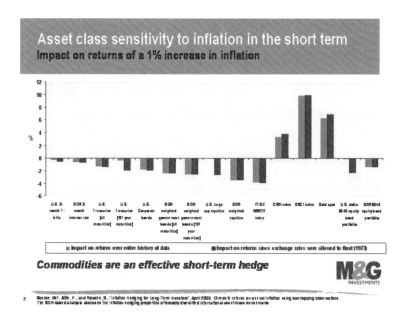

The attached chart shows the effects on nominal returns of various asset classes for a 1 percentage point increase in the rate of inflation over a one-year period. The results tend to be more conclusive for the post-Bretton Woods period since 1973. As you can see, all the major asset classes are assessed and all suffer after an increase in inflation, except commodities.

As Attie and Roache point out, "for long-term investors, a 12-month horizon is likely to be too short". The lads use a long-run model to assess whether the returns exhibited in the short-run by asset classes are similar over a longer period (20 years).

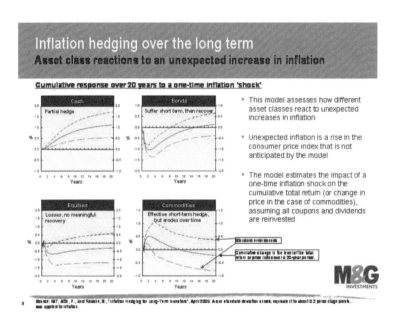

In the attached chart, an elasticity of 1 indicates that the asset class provides a perfect hedge against inflation shocks and that real returns for the various indices remain unchanged.

The authors find that over a 20-year period, "cash returns do increase in response to an inflation shock, but the response is very gradual and less than full... Over time, cash begins to recover on an inflation-adjusted basis, but this process plays out over a very long period". As discussed above, the move towards inflation targeting by central banks may mean that cash returns are more sensitive to inflation than has historically been the case.

Long-term treasury returns get whacked by inflation, as we would expect. Interestingly, these losses tend to peak around the 3 year mark of the 20-year time horizon with real return losses of nearly 2 percentage points. After this peak, yields and prices eventually stabilise and returns from treasuries improve due to higher running yields.

The authors find that the inflation shock is "likely to lead to higher long-term real yields, increasing the total return of bonds once the effects of the shock have been fully priced-in". Additionally, the bond coupon is reinvested and bonds mature at higher yields. A bond investor doesn't get fooled again after buying the bonds at low yields and inflation comes back.

With the risk of sounding like a one-eyed bond guy, I think I will directly quote Attie and Roache regarding equities:

"Equity returns decline in the months following an inflation shock and do not experience a meaningful recovery thereafter, leaving them as the worst performing asset class in our sample. After 1 year, equity returns are... 0.9% lower in real terms due to the inflation shock and the decline in returns bottoms out after about 3 years... [for a] 3% loss in real terms... Our findings are consistent with evidence from a range of earlier studies and add further weight to the evidence against the theoretical arguments for equities as a real asset class providing inflation protection when inflation is rising."

The authors note that "this result does not imply that equities underperform inflation over the very long run; indeed there is ample evidence that equities outperform other traditional asset classes in real terms over long horizons".

We think that what really matters for equity returns in an inflationary environment is the type of inflation an economy is facing. Is it demand-pull or cost-push inflation? In general, inflation is caused by demand-pull rather than cost-push factors. Demand-pull inflation is a sustained increase in the prices of goods and services resulting from high demand. No one is worried about economies overheating at the moment and thus demand-pull inflation. Arguably economies like Europe and the UK are facing cost-push inflation with the main cause being rising taxes and imported inflation. In an environment of cost-push inflation like the early 1970s, equity returns tend to suffer.

And whilst commodities do very well over the short-term, they tend to suffer over the long-term as the effects of inflation causes commodity prices to fall gradually over time. Commodity prices begin to fall, normally after a period of 2 years. Some reasons put forward for this relationship are that prices fall as supply comes on-stream, or demand for commodities is reduced because of higher interest rates or a business cycle slowdown.

Attie and Roache conclude that these findings have major implications for long-term investors, particularly if those investors have strong views about the path of inflation. In the words of the authors, "This is particularly true for "non-consensus" views in which investors may expect inflation surprises, whether positive or negative".

Again, on equities I will leave it to the lads to express their conclusion:

"Our results suggest that for investors who do not take tactical portfolio positions, the rationale for holding equities should be based on a very long-term horizon to ensure that the effects of inflation cycles average out. Investors with the scope to tilt their portfolios could underweight equities relative to their strategic benchmark in anticipation of higher inflation, but it may be more efficient to use other assets given their stronger and more consistent reactions".

The paper is fairly damning for those who think they can inflation-hedge an investment portfolio: "among traditional asset classes, inflation hedges are imperfect at best and unlikely to work at worst".

So what can investors do about protecting themselves from inflation?

Index-linked bonds (both government and corporate) are the only "traditional" asset class that will protect investors from inflation provided they hold the bond to maturity. As a buy and hold strategy, linkers work great. Because both the coupon payments and principal are adjusted in line with movements in a price index, an investor will be fully hedged against inflation (again – provided they hold the bond to maturity). Be warned – government linkers tend to be long duration securities, with the average UK and European linker having a duration of 15 and 8 years respectively. So investors have a lot of interest-rate risk in owning these bonds. Corporate linkers tend to have a shorter duration profile and it is important to have some short duration linkers in a portfolio as well. Don't forget that there are also trading costs and there will be some price volatility as investors' expectations for inflation change.

Inflation derivatives like swaps and options will also do the job, but it should be noted the markets for these derivatives are in infancy and considerably less liquid.

All in all, a very interesting paper that the pundits should try and get their heads around. It is one thing to look at a long-run chart of returns of the various asset classes through history, quite another to try and protect a portfolio of investments from future inflation.

Disclaimer – I don't want to be accused of stealth marketing because that is not what the bondvigilantes blog is about, so here is a blog that Jim wrote about the launch of a couple of funds that aim at protecting investors from inflation. For what it is worth, we don't think inflation is an issue over the medium term but think it will be sticky in 2011. Check out our views on inflation here.

Chapter 73
(Fiscal) rules are there to be broken

Anthony Doyle - Tuesday, February 15th, 2011

A fiscal rule is a permanent constraint on fiscal policy through simple numerical limits on budgetary aggregates. The purpose of fiscal rules is to force governments into responsible fiscal behaviour at a time when it may not be in that government's short term interests. Both the EU and the UK experimented with fiscal rules until the great financial crisis hit. Then all the rules flew out the window.

The twenty members of the European Economic and Monetary Union (EMU) are subject to the Stability and Growth Pact (SGP). Within the SGP, the member countries are expected to commit to three fiscal rules: the general government fiscal deficit is to be less than three percent of GDP; gross government debt is to be less than 60 percent of GDP; and the general government fiscal deficit should be close to balance or in surplus over the economic cycle. The Maastricht criteria were put in place for EU member states joining the EMU. The SGP was meant to ensure that European nations continue to observe the Maastricht criteria after they join the EMU.

In the UK, the "Code for Fiscal Stability" was passed into law in 1998 and contained a number of budgetary rules. The golden rule is over the economic cycle, the government will only borrow to invest and not to fund current spending. The sustainable investment rule states the public sector net debt as a proportion of GDP will be held over the economic cycle at a stable and prudent level. The government defined this level as 40 percent of GDP. The permanent balance rule indicates that tax revenues are planned to be a constant share of GDP, the permanent tax rate or share. This share is the lowest constant share of tax revenues in GDP that would ensure the long-run solvency of the government. The Code does allow the UK government to depart from the rules, as long as it gives a rationale for its decision.

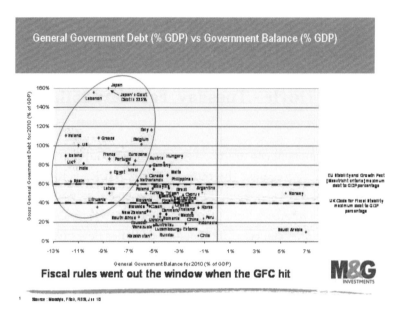

Fiscal rules went out the window when the GFC hit

This chart shows that governments broke their own fiscal rules in order to support their respective economies and financial systems. There are now a number of countries that are in real danger territory. How they will get themselves out of the mess they have found themselves in is anyone's guess.

In the UK, the government has formally suspended the rules and replaced them with a commitment to improve the government's finances when the economy returns to a positive economic growth rate. In Europe, the SGP is being reformed but not to everyone's satisfaction. Axel Weber (Head of Germany's Bundesbank until April 30) has called for more consistent sanctions on any breach of the rules and a swift consolidation of European government budget deficits.

It is notoriously difficult to enforce fiscal rules. It is not possible to fine governments as they may exacerbate the issue that the government is being fined for and would be counterproductive. Potential enforcers of fiscal rules are the investors in government debt and credit rating agencies. If fiscal rules are broken and investors and credit rating agencies become sufficiently concerned about the sustainability of the government's finances, it will have a large impact on the cost of capital through rising bond yields. Additionally, the government may find it hard to raise finance completely from capital markets as has been the case recently in Ireland and Greece. These countries have also had their respective credit ratings downgraded on concerns about the possibility of a debt restructuring event.

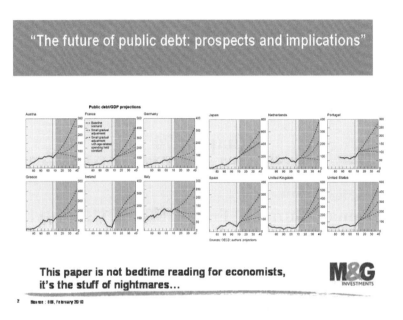

"The future of public debt: prospects and implications"

Public debt/GDP projections

This paper is not bedtime reading for economists, it's the stuff of nightmares...

M&G INVESTMENTS

2 Source : BIS, February 2010

In February 2010, the BIS released a working paper entitled "The future of public debt: prospects and implications". The attached chart shows 30 year projections for the debt/GDP ratio in a dozen major industrial economies. The large deterioration in debt figures is the result of rapidly aging populations and unfunded liabilities stemming from future age-related spending in these countries. The red line represents the baseline scenario, the green line represents a gradual improvement of government finances, and the blue line represents the draconian policy of cutting future age-related liabilities (an incumbent government would have to be bonkers to do such a thing!). The paper does not offer any advice on how to tackle the looming fiscal dangers but does note: "a decision to raise the retirement age appears a better measure than a future cut in benefits or an increase in taxes". This is an interesting thought. In 20 years time, will the retirement age be 70, 75, 80?

It tends to be the case that governments faced with reducing government spending, cut potentially beneficial investment plans rather than current spending. Not good. As we all know, a newly elected government often has a tendency to abandon the previous government's announced policies. As mentioned previously on this blog, it may be the case that newly elected governments in countries like Ireland and Greece will choose to abandon the fiscal austerity plans of the previous government. This could have a massive impact not only on their respective economies but also on bond markets.

Chapter 74
Iceland and its banks – a blueprint for Europe?

Tamara Burnell - Friday, March 11th, 2011

Much has been written about Iceland's response to its banking crisis, and whether its decision to put its banks into administration and swiftly force losses onto bank creditors has proved to be the key to restoring economic stability. Does this provide a model that Ireland and others should have followed? Commentators such as Paul Krugman (see this link http://nyti.ms/fQXFIT) and the IMF were quick to point out that Icelandic GDP expanded by 2.2% in Q3 2010, setting it firmly on the path to recovery, though the subsequent 1.5% contraction in Q4 showed that Iceland's problems were far from fully resolved. While it's hard to place too much weight on notoriously volatile Icelandic macroeconomic data, given the small size of the economy (with a population of just 319,000, a single factory closure or even just a few families catching a nasty cold could materially influence output), it is worth digging beneath the surface to find out what is really going on as there are still some interesting lessons for the rest of Europe.

So what did Iceland do apart from putting the banks into administration? For a start, they were quick to prioritise national interests above obligations to other European countries, most notably in refusing to compensate the UK and Netherlands for the bail-out of Icesave depositors. While I am not arguing that this was in any way morally correct, it certainly did give politicians the breathing space needed to work on other measures, both by reducing the national debt burden and by giving citizens some say in their future. A further referendum on the subject is due in April, after previous compromise measures were firmly rejected by the Icelandic population (given the amounts involved, the outcome of these negotiations will be critical for Iceland's debt position). Of course, it is much harder for the peripheral Eurozone countries to simply ignore the EU demands that their citizens honour not just their sovereign debt but also their banking sector liabilities to avoid banks in core Europe (and the ECB) having to crystallise losses on their periphery exposures. But equally it will be hard for elected governments in the periphery to maintain the long term support of their populations for the austerity measures needed to repay all the bank and sovereign liabilities if they don't give their citizens some sort of say in the matter.

Secondly, Iceland was both willing, and, crucially, able, to embark on a comprehensive restructuring of other debts within the financial system, not just bank liabilities. Debt levels of households and corporates were also unsustainable, and simply writing off bank liabilities was never going to be enough to reduce the overall leverage of the country. The popularity of inflation linked mortgages in Iceland meant that when the currency collapsed in the wake of the banking crisis, and the soaring cost of imports caused inflation to spike close to 20%, a large proportion of the population found themselves unable to service their mortgages. Similarly, a large number of corporate and consumer loans had been denominated in foreign currency, and the collapse of the Icelandic krona meant that these loans also created a heavy burden on borrowers. Like several other countries, Iceland proposed mortgage forgiveness, allowing for partial write offs of debts and capping loans at 110% LTV to limit negative equity. However, unlike other countries, Iceland also attempted to clarify how the inevitable losses would be shared; partly by the newly created (and primarily state and creditor owned) banks, partly by the state's housing fund, and partly by the insurance and pension funds who had invested in Icelandic mortgages. After long wrangling with the IMF, it appears the basic principles of this restructuring agreement have been agreed by all sides, though the devil will of course be in the detail.

This ability to get savers and borrowers around the table together to hammer out a burden sharing agreement is critical – of course it is much easier in a small country, especially once foreign creditors have already been snubbed, but it's a process that I believe other countries will have to go through. The politics are also much simpler in a country with a relatively young population, where borrowers outweigh savers – countries with different demographics and a strong savings and pensions sector will find it much harder to implement debt forgiveness measures. However, ultimately they may have to try. Interestingly, Hungary has set a precedent for dealing with recalcitrant private pension funds by effectively nationalising them, and while a drastic solution, it is not unthinkable that similar measures could be implemented elsewhere in the EU if that is what is needed to bring all creditors to the table.

Finally, in the wake of the crisis, Iceland imposed capital controls to prevent the flow of funds offshore. While this has costs to the population, particularly savers stuck with devalued krona savings, it has proved useful in enabling the government to fund its budget domestically. Again, this sort of measure wouldn't be easy for Eurozone countries to implement unilaterally, but in a country such as Ireland where the banking sector is effectively state owned, it would be interesting to see whether capital controls could to some extent be achieved via administrative measures.

The jury is still out on whether Iceland's restructuring will ultimately be successful, and as highlighted above it will be tricky for Eurozone members to implement the same measures, but Iceland certainly provides an interesting case study in dealing with a financial crisis.

Chapter 75
An update on the impact of the VAT rises in the UK compared to Australia and Japan

Jim Leaviss - Monday, March 28th, 2011

Here's an update of a slide we produced a year ago following the January 2010 move back to 17.5% VAT from the 15% emergency rate. We were comparing the UK's retail sales numbers to those in Australia and Japan around the time of their consumption tax hikes, and asking whether we'd see pre-loading of purchases ahead of the sales tax and a collapse back afterwards. The blue line shows that there was some deterioration in sales post the tax rise, but it was probably not as pronounced as we might have expected.

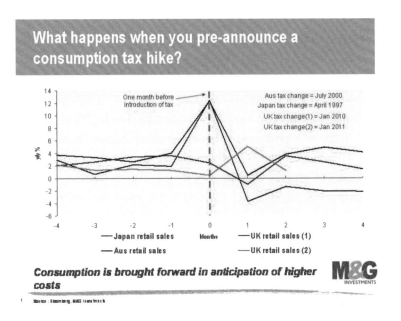

What happens when you pre-announce a consumption tax hike?

Consumption is brought forward in anticipation of higher costs

M&G INVESTMENTS

With a move up in VAT again, this time to 20%, we can see how things are going this year. Remember that December's weather was pretty grim, and that the VAT hike was on 4th January – so there was pent up demand post Christmas and 3 days of shopping in January before the hike came in. We can see that sales rose in January – which wasn't in the script! Last week though we saw the release of February's official retail sales data showing a fall of 0.8% compared with January. Department store sales were especially weak (down 3.2% on the month). If we see a similar pattern to last year, we could expect the year on year rate of retail sales growth to turn negative hereafter.

The VAT hike might actually turn out to be relatively trivial to consumers in the scheme of things. Whilst sales fell, shops saw the biggest increases in prices (the deflator) for years – this was the biggest month on month increase in the price deflator since the series began in 1988, and only a part of this was due to the VAT rise. Clothing and footwear inflation was especially strong. The next few months could be very tough for retailers.

Chapter 76
Icelandic geysers say "No"

Richard Woolnough - Tuesday, April 12th, 2011

Last weekend the voters of Iceland said no to honouring claims made against their nation by the British and Dutch governments. These claims originate from the failure of "IceSave" saving accounts. Many depositors in these accounts were based in the UK and Holland. In the wake of the funding crisis the UK and Dutch governments covered the losses of their respective citizens.

The Icelandics are faced with a dilemma. Do they choose the cheap short-term option of walking away from their debt, or the expensive short-term option of paying up? If they choose the latter, then Iceland will probably garner greater support in terms of future potential borrowing, and a higher possibility of joining the EU club.

It is likely that the next stage of the IceSave process will be in court, and this shows the dilemma of lending to a state as opposed to a corporation. Even if the court rules against Iceland, how will the UK and Dutch governments recover their money? Default risk is lower in sovereign credits than corporates, but recovery is often at the whim of the electorate, and rightly so. Most sovereign states have the benefit of democratic constitutions. When lending to a corporation it is the probability of default and recovery potential that investors have to focus on. When lending to a sovereign it is the willingness and ability of the citizens to repay debt that investors have to focus on.

The claim from the UK and the Dutch is a result of them bowing to their own electorate who had invested with Icelandic institutions, and they were given their money back in full, despite the deposit protection scheme being well publicised. In this case, we have the bizarre situation where a company operating outside its national boundaries has defaulted, the voting members of the sovereign state they operate in get bailed out, and the claim is passed onto another state, whose electorate (not surprisingly) do not wish to pay.

The Icelandic voters have decided they did not want to bail out the UK and Dutch governments, who had bailed out their own voters. Given the structure of the Eurozone banking system, one currency, hugely mobile capital, and a multitude of democracies, Iceland could well be a test case of what happens next (see previous blog on Iceland here). Financial integration without political integration plain and simply will not work.

Chapter 77
Career opportunities – the ones that never knock. With youth unemployment rising steadily in the UK, where are the protest songs?

Jim Leaviss - Friday, May 13th, 2011

"Wham, bam – I am, a man

Job or no job, you can't tell me that I'm not.

Hey everybody take a look at me

I've got street credibility

I may not have a job but I have a good time

With the boys that I meet down on the line."

"Wham Rap" by Wham!, 1982

My mate told me recently that the first Wham! album was surprisingly good, so I bought it. It is good, and I am surprised. I was also surprised to find how political songs like Wham Rap were, and it got me thinking about writing a blog about the political songs that made the charts in the 1980s in response to the recession, and wondering why today's youth haven't written any. After all, youth unemployment is famously high isn't it?

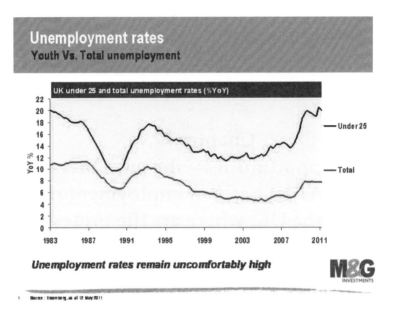

The data only goes back to 1983 for youth unemployment – but you can see that the early 80s were a time of youth unemployment rates of nearly 20%. In 1981 we had songs like Ghost Town by the Specials, 1 in 10 by UB40 (the band itself named after the dole claim form), Shipbuilding by Elvis Costello in 1982, and by 1985 Frankie Goes to Hollywood were selling T-Shirts saying "Frankie Say Arm the Unemployed" and leading a delegation to Downing Street to deliver a petition against the axeing of benefits for school leavers if they didn't go onto a Youth Training Scheme (YTS). It was signed by Paul Weller, Madness, Smiley Culture, the Flying Pickets (another politically relevant name inspired by the miners' strike) and Alison Moyet.

Some argue that the youth unemployment numbers are distorted (this post http://bit.ly/ewwkJP on the website Straight Statistics says that the treatment of youths in education is a distorting factor, and that the outright number of young people claiming unemployment benefits is little different than it was in the early 1990s, although it was high then too). Nevertheless there are 1.7 million people between the ages of 18 and 24 who are economically inactive (of which 0.7 million are officially unemployed, the remainder are largely in education). If anything, with free tertiary education a thing of the past (although with access to that education easier) the kids of today have even more to be aggrieved about – those going to university are being saddled with debts of tens of thousands of pounds. And never before has the technology to make music (or indeed film) been so cheap and available. I've a grand piano, a drum machine, and an 8 track recording studio on my mobile phone. Maybe you can only be a protest singer if you have an acoustic guitar. Incidentally whilst thinking about this issue I stumbled across an article on the BBC website, by an American writer wondering where the great US cultural response to the Great Financial Crisis is. Perhaps, he speculates, the safety net is greater than it once was, and the starting point for living standards higher thanks to multi-income families?

Perhaps though there are protest songs out there but I'm missing them? Let me know.

On an unrelated note, I was in Ireland seeing clients earlier this week – one recommended I read this article by Morgan Kelly, a notorious economics professor at University College Dublin, from Saturday's Irish Times. In it he claims that the Central Bank governor Patrick Honohan's decision to keep a government guarantee on Irish bank bonds was "the costliest mistake ever made by an Irish person". He says that the only way to avoid an Irish sovereign bond default is to effectively default on the ECB loans made to the Irish banking sector, halving Ireland's debt to Euro 110 billion. He also thinks government borrowing needs to fall to zero. Neither of these outcomes looks likely – Irish CDS currently trades at 640 bps and there is open talk about default being both acceptable and even desirable. The mood is relentlessly gloomy in Dublin – our taxi driver told us that his firm now hires him out at a daily rate of Euro 200 compared with Euro 440 a couple of years ago. There's no shortage of taxis – it's a service where demand collapses simultaneously with a dramatic increase in supply as people try to earn an extra income.

Finally, and totally unrelated to bond markets or economics, the film How to Lose Friends and Alienate People was on TV earlier this week. This is the story of Toby Young (who is trying to set up a Free School near where I live in Hammersmith – don't get me started…) and his disastrous time on the staff of Vanity Fair in New York working for the famous editor Graydon Carter. It reminded me that I read the book when it first came out, and finished it on a plane. I'd never heard of Graydon Carter before, but as I disembarked the man in front of me's tennis racket case dangled in my face revealing a business card tag stating "Graydon Carter, Vanity Fair". What are the chances of that? Then I realised that whilst for me, the chances of being on a flight with him were minutely small, the chance of Graydon Carter being on the same flight as somebody reading that newly published book were probably evens or better.

Chapter 78
NS&I Index Linked Certificates – a government subsidy for rich savers

Jim Leaviss - Monday, May 16th, 2011

Get `em while they're hot. The new National Savings inflation linked certificates were launched on Thursday last week, to great rejoicing on the money pages of the newspapers. And rightly so – these are a gimme. Although the rate of interest (RPI + 0.5%) is lower than on the similar certificates withdrawn 10 months ago (RPI +1%), this is still attractive compared to the market rate for 5 year real yields. With the same government credit risk, the 2016 index-linked gilt yields RPI minus 0.5%, i.e. a 1% lower yield than these retail only certificates. AND the NS&I product is tax free! So for taxpayers the yields are outstanding. With the breakeven inflation rate on the 2016 linker at just 2.9% on an RPI basis, so maybe at 1.9% on a CPI basis, this implies inflation below the Bank of England target level on average over the next 5 years, and the absolute level looks good too.

Why is the government offering such an attractive product? It's giving 50% taxpayers an AAA rated, riskless investment equivalent to nearly 10% at current levels of RPI and about 7% if inflation averages 3% over the period. I can't even find many junk bonds that pay 10% nowadays. And this is happening whilst the banks and building societies are desperate for retail funding – this is "£2 billion that the private sector won't be able to raise and lend to first time buyers and homeowners" (says the Building Societies Association).

Well I guess the first reason is that it needs the money. The NS&I has to contribute £14 bn towards funding the deficit this financial year, and this will certainly help. But did the rate need to be so generous, and so far from the market rate? The government has talked about these certificates in terms of helping the poor savers stuck in low yielding bank accounts. But those with savings to benefit from this deal are largely the richest portion of society – many of those will be higher rate taxpayers who have been given a windfall gain. Is this a deliberate subsidy for the rich?

I'd also have thought that the government might have taken the opportunity to move to a CPI+ basis rather than continuing to use RPI. After all, that's the BoE's target, and pension funds are being encouraged to move to using CPI for their liabilities too. With the "wedge" between RPI and CPI high, and likely to be about 1% going forward that might have been a smart thing to have done – although there would have been some negative press headline risk in doing so.

I talked to Richard Woolnough about this being a windfall giveaway for the rich – a kind of subsidy from the government. He pointed out that these certificates have been available under the last Labour government too, and we doubted that a subsidy for the rich was their explicit policy. But he also made a good point that there is another government subsidy for rich savers – the deposit protection scheme that allows a huge amount of savings to be guaranteed by HMG if you spread it around the market below the £85,000 ceiling for individual banks. This, like the huge interest on the latest inflation certificates, is a real cost to the taxpayer – as the bailout of Northern Rock showed. Another example of the baby boom generation writing itself generous promises for which the poor youth of today will end up funding?

Chapter 79
UK inflation shocking?

Mike Riddell - Tuesday, May 17th, 2011

UK CPI inflation jumped from 4.0% to 4.5%, versus expectations of only a slight increase to 4.1%. Core CPI, which strips out food and energy prices, soared from 3.2% to 3.7% and is now at easily a record high (data goes back to 1997). One bank called the inflation numbers shocking, arguing other economies aren't seeing anything like this surge in core inflation, UK monetary policy is too loose and the MPC should hike rates in August.

The first thing to point out, as previously discussed on this blog (see this link http://bit.ly/rMWKa0), is that the CPI figures include the VAT increase to 20% in January. The VAT increase is presumably temporary unless there's another hike next year, and will therefore fall out of the inflation numbers early next year (it's difficult to say exactly when as it depends on the timing and extent of the VAT passthrough from retailers to consumers). This chart gives a truer 'long term' picture of UK inflation by stripping out this tax effect, and as you can see, 2.8% is still within the Bank of England's target (albeit energy and food price increases over the past year have pulled it uncomfortably close to 3%). Note that the headline CPI number came in temporarily lower than the constant tax measure through 2009 following the VAT cut in January of that year, but the last two years have seen the headline CPI inflation number look temporarily high.

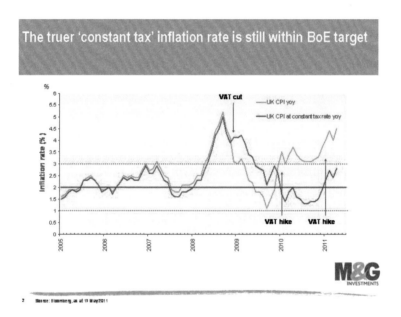

The truer 'constant tax' inflation rate is still within BoE target

The second thing to point out is that even if inflation does continue rising through this year (and maybe unexpectedly fails to fall next year), will the Bank of England really hike rates? Well the market seems to think so, as it's still pricing in two 0.25% rate hikes in the UK by this time next year, with the first hike coming in November.

However this chart shows just how badly wrong the market has got its UK interest rate forecasts. Each dotted line shows the market's expectations of the future course of the Bank of England base rate at the time of each quarterly inflation report going back to August 2009. In August 2009, the market was pricing in a Bank of England Bank Rate for May 2011 of 3.25%. Instead, the Bank Rate has remained firmly stuck at 0.5%. It's all the more surprising if you consider that UK inflation has consistently exceeded market expectations at the time of release, so if inflation is the primary driver of the Bank Rate, you'd have expected to see the market <u>underestimate</u> the Bank Rate over this period.

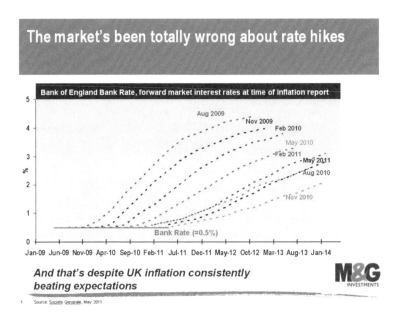

Why has the market been so wrong? The answer is all about growth – investors have placed too much emphasis on inflation in their Bank Rate forecasts. The UK economy is no bigger than it was six months ago. UK consumption has flatlined. With such a vulnerable consumer, housing market, and banking sector, we can't risk higher rates. With that in mind, it's not a bad idea to have a fresh look at the second part of the opening paragraph in the Bank of England's quarterly Inflation Report:

'In order to maintain price stability, the Government has set the Bank's Monetary Policy Committee (MPC) a target for the annual inflation rate of the Consumer Prices Index of 2%. Subject to that, the MPC is also required to support the Government's objective of maintaining high and stable growth and employment.'

Chapter 80
More on the impact of inflation on equities

James Thompson - Thursday, May 26th, 2011

A few months ago, Anthony wrote about inflation hedging (see this link http://bit.ly/rtwTc9) and referred to an IMF paper which suggested that 'traditional asset classes', most notably equities, don't fare well if inflation increases, which is something to bear in mind when trying to protect a portfolio against increases in the level of prices.

Francesco Curto at Deutsche Bank recently released a research piece that comes to similar conclusions. The article states that investors regularly use equities as an inflation hedge because of the view that nominal earnings and dividends rise faster when inflation is high, but this was not the case in the US during the 1970's. Deutsche Bank show that over the last 50 years, while nominal returns on equity rose, real returns on equity actually fell.

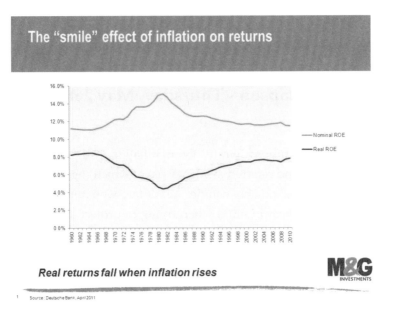

Deutsche's research also shows that a fall in the PE ratio should be expected as inflation rises. For investors to be protected against inflation free cash flow would need to grow in line with inflation. If equities were a perfect inflation hedge, ceteris paribus, then the PE ratio should remain unchanged as the share price and corporate earnings increase in line with inflation. The article does suggest that inflation hedging with equities may be possible, but due to the depressed levels of PE it could prove to be more costly than expected.

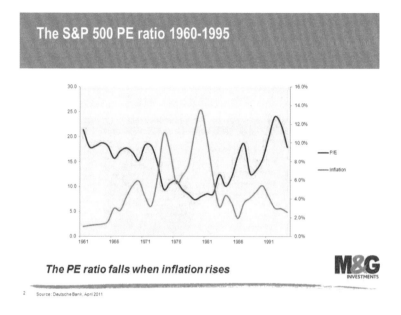

The PE ratio falls when inflation rises

Source: Deutsche Bank, April 2011

Looks like bond investors and central banks aren't the only ones that need to keep a close eye on inflation.

Chapter 81
Stockholm syndrome: UK consumers love their supermarkets even as food inflation runs at nearly 2.5 times that in Europe

Jim Leaviss - Thursday, June 2nd, 2011

Why is UK inflation running at a much higher rate than European inflation? The UK's CPI is 4.5% compared with 2.7% in Europe. One answer might be food inflation, a major portion of the overall CPI baskets (11% in the UK, 15% in the Eurozone – add in alcohol and both are a little higher).

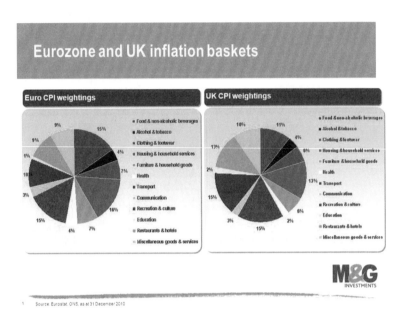

The chart shows that the UK rate of food inflation is systematically higher than that in Europe. At the moment the year on year increase is 4.7% compared with 2%, and at times the difference has been much higher. There are times when you might explain this through £ weakness feeding into imported food prices, but the chart includes periods of both currency strength and weakness. What else might explain structurally higher food inflation in the UK?

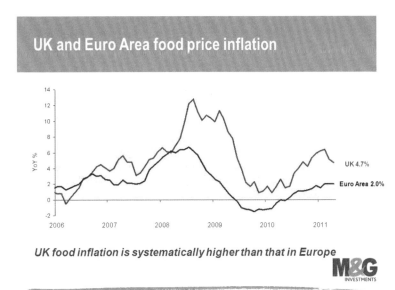

UK and Euro Area food price inflation

UK 4.7%

Euro Area 2.0%

UK food inflation is systematically higher than that in Europe

M&G
INVESTMENTS

2   Source: Bloomberg, as at 30 April 2011

Well the chart from Mark Capleton of SocGen might be at least part of the answer. It shows earnings per share (EPS) growth for UK and European food retailers. When food price inflation started to moderate post the last shock in 2008, European food retailers cut prices. In the UK the supermarkets realised that they had pricing power and kept raising them; this resulted in the strong relative profitability that they enjoyed. There might be other factors involved – the UK supermarkets have massively diversified into non-food goods (everything from clothing to DVDs to insurance), but it does look like UK consumers are being hit by the lack of competition in the food retail sector.

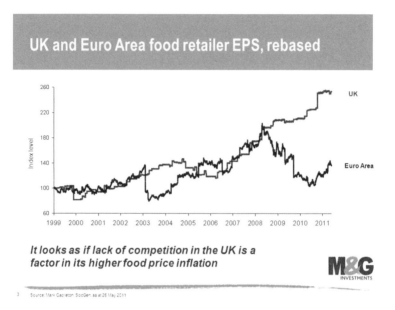

It looks as if lack of competition in the UK is a factor in its higher food price inflation

This BBC Watchdog survey from 2009 shows that only 2% of respondents were "very dissatisfied" with their supermarket (about half were actively "very satisfied"). Yet they claim that price is the most important thing in their choice of shop. Stockholm Syndrome is a "paradoxical psychological phenomenon wherein hostages express empathy and have positive feelings towards their captors".

Chapter 82
Greece and the Deathly Hallows

Richard Woolnough - Monday, July 18th, 2011

This weekend's family activity centred on the final film in the Harry Potter series, Harry Potter and the Deathly Hallows, 10 years on from when we saw the first instalment of the magical film series in 2001. Meanwhile in the Monday to Friday muggle world, the markets are focusing on the modern classical tale of Greece, that also began 10 years ago in 2001 when they entered the European Monetary Union. How will that blockbuster story end?

In the final instalment of Harry Potter, the story centres on the deathly hallows. Spookily, the three elements of the deathly hallows are comparable to some of the magical instruments Greece has at its disposal.

Sadly, they have already used the invisibility cloak to hide the true extent of their debt, in order to gain entry into the Eurozone back in 2001. Unfortunately, for them that magical charm has been exposed and its protection is lost. This leaves them with two further deathly hallows to get them through their current nightmare. They could use the resurrection stone, i.e. they can default and their debt will reappear as a shadow of its former self, remaining in the Euro, but angering the European Central Bank, and investors. Alternately, they could take the option of using the elder wand to threaten to destroy the whole system, and therefore gain support from fellow Eurozone members to band together to keep their debt whole, the Eurozone dream alive, and the European Central Bank happy. Both give very different economic and bond outcomes. Their fate however, like in the Potter series, is not just in their hands but that of their friends and adversaries.

So what other spells can the participants in this economic fable use? The Greeks would love to cast the *"Evanesco"* spell (makes the target vanish). This would involve full economic union and therefore making the Greek debt really disappear – a perfect outcome for Greece, unlike the previous attempt to hide it under the invisibility cloak. The Ministry of Magic, better known in the muggle world as the IMF, would love to use its usual magical curse of *"Crucio"* (inflicts unbearable pain on the recipient of the curse), insisting the over indulgent borrower amends its ways. Hard for the Greeks to bear, but would have the support of the houses of the north. A third potential conclusion to the tale would involve the casting by the invisible hand of the markets (or as politicians might term it, the death eaters) of the appropriately named *"Expulso"* (a spell that causes an object to explode), the Greeks leave, or are expelled from the Euro, with the potential disorderly reintroduction of a new national currency by the Greek authorities.

Like in this weekend's movie, battles and losses lie ahead under all scenarios. We think that the *"Expulso"* conclusion as touched on previously is the likely final denouement. If it happens, it will be very painful in the short term unlike the other options, but in the long term the natural order of national economic stability would emerge as nation states and markets would set domestically appropriate exchange rates, fiscal and monetary policies, thus allowing the efficient distribution of labour and capital, and hopefully an eventual happy ending.

Chapter 83
Forget stress tests – ring fencing banks from sovereigns is the real issue

Tamara Burnell - Tuesday, July 19th, 2011

So the results of the bank stress tests are out. Do they add anything from an investor viewpoint?

Well, despite the best efforts of the European Banking Authority, we didn't get the harmonised EU data we were hoping for. To say that there are inconsistencies in the data would be an understatement.

Disclosure varies hugely bank by bank, especially in areas such as their Loan to Value ratios for real estate lending, and that's before you start trying to factor in the differences in the way property valuations are performed or indexed in each country. Banks, and in particular the tax systems and legal systems in which they operate, are still national. We're a long way from a harmonised, EU wide banking sector.

There's also no real information on banks' liquidity positions. Assumed funding cost increases over the next two years are simply driven by the interest rate assumptions used, with little or no linkage to the banks' actual and increasing costs of funding. It's impossible to analyse what is happening to individual banks' funding sources and costs. The EBA admits liquidity and funding is a critical issue but has backed away from making public its liquidity stress testing, presumably because they are concerned this might provoke further concerns.

One of the most frustrating issues for investors is that the EBA doesn't stress test the legal entities to which investors and market counterparties are exposed or potentially exposed. So the French mutual groups are tested on a consolidated basis, when in fact debt and equity investors are taking exposure to very specific legal entities within the group, such as CASA within the Credit Agricole group, whose risk profile will be very different to that of the consolidated group.

However, the most important statement from the EBA in our view was the instruction to national regulators to require banks to raise core capital by any means possible, "including where necessary restrictions on dividends, deleveraging, issuance of fresh capital or **conversion of lower quality instruments into Core Tier 1 capital.**"

This means conversion of debt into equity where other sources of equity are unavailable. In Ireland this has already been accepted as necessary but in most EU countries regulators still do not have the legal powers to push through a forcible debt for equity conversion. Banks could of course try to achieve this via voluntary conversions, but ultimately the incentive for bondholders to agree to a conversion is limited unless there is the very real threat of a more draconian resolution regime to act as a "stick".

Regulators and governments alike are well aware of this issue. The Financial Stability Board will this week put forward a consultation paper on the subject of international resolution regimes, along similar lines to the EU consultation published in January. These proposals aim to ensure governments can't be forced to bail out the banking sector and thereby to ringfence the sovereign's finances from those of its banks.

Equally, the critical issue of private sector burden sharing by the banks in any sovereign debt default also remains unsolved – until we get a clear framework for clarifying the role of banks in investing in sovereign debt, and find a mechanism for ensuring that all creditors, including banks, can and do take losses on investments in insolvent sovereigns, the umbilical cord between banks and sovereigns remains intact.

So rather than waste time sifting through stress test result spreadsheets, investors would be advised to analyse and understand the FSB resolution regime proposals for banks and the European Stability Mechanism framework for private sector burden sharing on sovereign debt. These are the critical issues facing investors right now, and all the stress tests do is highlight how important it is that a solution is found to enable banks and sovereigns to ringfence themselves from each other.

(For those interested in how the results might differ had sovereign debt haircuts been taken into consideration, see this calculator from Reuters Breakingviews http://reut.rs/rndoUe .)

Chapter 84
A light in the storm – the German economic boom

Anthony Doyle - Thursday, July 28th, 2011

There is a shining light amidst the storm of the European sovereign debt crisis. Europe's largest economy, Germany, is booming. Since June 2009, the German Federal Statistical Office has had the pleasure of notifying financial markets that the German unemployment rate has fallen. Today we received further confirmation of the strength of the German labour market, with the German unemployment rate remaining at a record low of 7.0%. This equates to a fall in unemployment of 11,000 in the month of July. In total, around 550,000 jobs have been created in the German economy since June 2009. Consequently, German consumer confidence is around record highs.

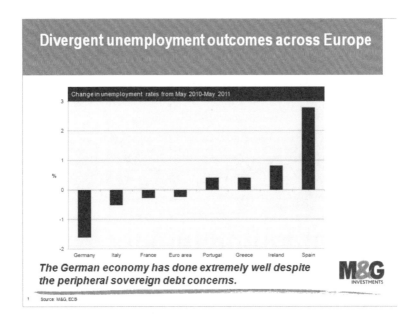

Divergent unemployment outcomes across Europe

Change in unemployment rates from May 2010-May 2011

The German economy has done extremely well despite the peripheral sovereign debt concerns.

1   Source: M&G, ECB

There are many reasons for the stellar performance of the German labour market. The German economy grew at 1.5% in the first quarter of 2011, or 4.9% over the year. Importantly, the growth numbers were mainly underpinned by strong domestic demand. Initially, the fall in the euro due to concerns over peripheral Europe provided the conditions for a boost in German exports. Now, the growth base has broadened, with domestic investment and consumption becoming increasingly supportive. It is our view that without the euro currency in place, the German Deutschmark would be the strongest currency in the world, German bunds may have negative yields, and the German economy would probably be in recession. The Swiss are experiencing this phenomenon through the strong appreciation of the Swiss franc in recent times. Is the Swiss franc a new safe haven?

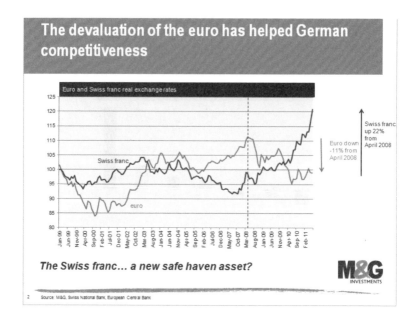

Of course, GDP is entirely backward looking. It is important that we also assess what the forward looking indicators are telling us as well. German business surveys are a good place to start. Despite the current concerns, German purchasing and manufacturing indices (PMIs) for both the manufacturing and services sector continue to suggest that the expansion of the German economy continued in Q2. It isn't the stellar growth experienced earlier in the year, but a growth rate of around 0.5% in Q2 isn't too bad considering the concerns around Greece. Despite the worries, the Ifo business climate and expectations index both suggest that the German corporate sector is in a relatively good mood. German firms are telling us that they are planning on spending record amounts on capital expenditure and investment in the coming 12 months as indicated by the German DIHK business survey. Consequently, it is not unreasonable to expect that the German labour market will continue to improve in coming months as firms look to invest in profitable projects.

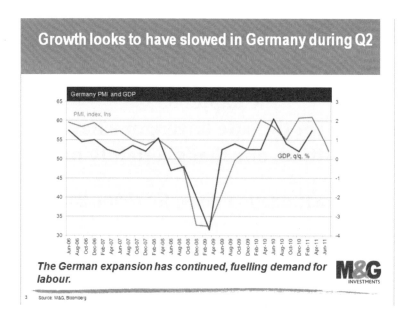

Growth looks to have slowed in Germany during Q2

Germany PMI and GDP

PMI, index, lhs

GDP, q/q, %

The German expansion has continued, fuelling demand for labour.

3   Source: M&G, Bloomberg

In a way, the strong German growth outcome is directly related to the peripheral sovereign woes. The euro is currently far too weak for Germany, which means that the German economy is extremely competitive, its economy is booming, and its inflation is starting to accelerate. This is why the ECB has been hiking rates and may hike again before the year is out. But the flip side of German growth is the utterly miserable growth rate in Southern Europe, which is because the euro is far too strong for these deeply uncompetitive economies. Fernanda Nechio, an economist at the Federal Reserve Bank of San Francisco, estimates interest rates based on a Taylor rule analysis for peripheral Europe and core Europe. Her analysis suggests an ECB target rate of around 3% for core Europe, and a target rate of around -3% for peripheral Europe. On the one hand, the ECB is hiking rates to tighten monetary policy for the stronger core European nations, and on the other it is retaining loose monetary policy by maintaining liquidity arrangements for the weak peripheral European banks.

Some might say, the German economic party is the result of the peripheral European economic funeral. The German public bailing out southern Europe is the cost that they need to pay for strong growth outcomes and rising standards of living. Bailing out peripheral Europe is like a tax that has until now been deferred. To quote Dolly Parton: "If you want the rainbow Germany, you sometimes have to put up with the rain".

Chapter 85
The quest for the safe haven; one haven that's justified, one that's certainly not

Mike Riddell - Friday, July 29th, 2011

A lot of the cash that's been created over the past few years is sloshing around the world trying to find somewhere to hide. There has been a huge bid for anything deemed a safe haven asset, a bid that has been propelled by an imploding Eurozone and US politicians that are seemingly looking to bring its $14 trillion poker game to a spectacular finale by committing collective hara-kiri.

The problem is that if you take the US out of the picture, there aren't enough non-shaky AAA assets to go around. Germany and France have about $1.7tn of sovereign debt outstanding, although France is probably the next AAA-rated country to find its credit rating under threat. The UK has about $1.2tn of sovereign debt, and gilts have been big beneficiaries recently, but a double dip recession in the UK (which MPC member Martin Weale recently highlighted as a risk) will cause a U-turn on austerity measures which in turn will place the UK's AAA rating at risk. After the UK, Canada has about $1 trillion of sovereign debt. After that you're pretty stuck – Australia has about $0.3tn, Sweden has $0.1tn, and there are a few countries with even less debt.

Norway is the safest sovereign in the world if you take the cost of insuring against default from the CDS market, but as you'd expect for the world's best quality sovereign, Norway has very little sovereign debt. As a result, the demand for Norwegian government bonds has massively outstripped supply, and a large gap has opened up between the yield on Norwegian government bonds and the Norwegian Krone 10 year swap rate. The difference between the cash rate and the swap rate is now at a similar level to that seen in October 2008. We think that the strong bid for government bonds issued by Norway, Sweden and

Germany is totally justified though – indeed, we've been filling our boots with the stuff over the past few months, and given our well documented ongoing nervousness regarding a number of sovereign states' creditworthiness, we think that there's still significant value in the safest AAA markets.

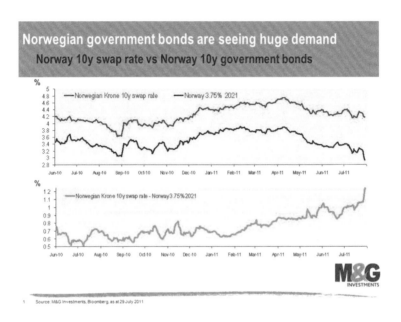

1   Source: M&G Investments, Bloomberg, as at 29 July 2011

The big safe haven bid has also been hitting some emerging markets, but in contrast to the money flying into Norwegian government bonds, the EM safe haven bid looks plain bonkers. The chart below shows the recent price action of Brazil's 30 year US dollar denominated government bond, where spreads over US Treasuries have tightened from 140 basis points at the beginning of June to under 100 basis points now. Credit ratings don't count for all that much these days, but if markets think a risk premium of less than 100 basis points is a fair price for a 30 year bond denominated in US dollars that is benchmarked over US Treasuries and is issued by a country that's rated one notch above junk status then the market's smoking crack.

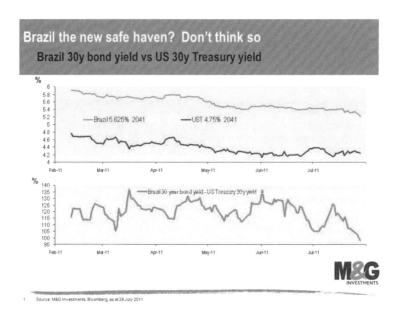

1   Source: M&G Investments, Bloomberg, as at 28 July 2011

This isn't to say that emerging markets as an asset class are poor value. Much of what has driven financial markets over the past 15 years has been a direct consequence of emerging market countries maintaining artificially undervalued exchange rates. The global current account imbalances that have resulted from these policies go a long way to explaining the behaviour of various asset classes over this period. These global imbalances have lessened since 2007, but they still persist. Developed countries need a sharp devaluation versus many of their emerging market counterparts to restore competitiveness, restore economic growth, and ultimately help reduce debt levels. Overheating emerging markets need their currencies to appreciate, and EM currencies should (with a few exceptions) continue to rally versus developed market currencies.

But buying long dated Brazilian US$ denominated bonds is not how to implement this view. We think that the implied default risk from a number of emerging market bonds is far too low – an implied default risk that has been squished by the huge flow of money into EM debt and a relative lack of supply – and we have selectively put on trades across a number of our bond funds that reflect the view that some areas of the hard currency EM debt market are getting dramatically overvalued.

Chapter 86
Oil prices and the impact on inflation linked bonds

Jim Leaviss - Wednesday, August 10th, 2011

With a significant fall in the oil price (-28% since the end of April), inflation linked bonds are underperforming their nominal counterparts. The biggest impact though is in the US market, where TIPS yields have risen, especially at the shorter maturities. This chart shows that whilst short dated index linked gilt yields have edged up in the last couple of weeks, the yield on the 2012 maturity TIPS has risen aggressively.

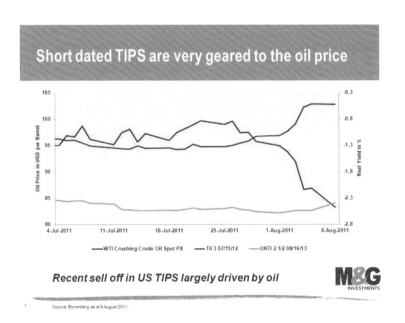

Source: Bloomberg, as at 9 August 2011

Why are oil prices (both rising and falling) much more important for US inflation linked bonds than they are for those in the UK and Europe? It's all about tax. In the UK, the duty rate for road fuel is the equivalent of £2.20 per US gallon, and VAT at 20% is charged on top of both the fuel and the duty. European taxes are similarly high (the Netherlands is especially high). In the US, federal tax is just 18.4 cents per gallon – adding in other state taxes, the average is 48.1 cents per gallon. So UK fuel taxes including VAT are about 10 times higher than those in the US. As a result, a rise or fall in the crude oil price impacts a much, much bigger part of the cost of a gallon of gasoline in the US than elsewhere, and therefore there is a more significant impact on the CPI as a result (both directly in the fuel element, and then subsequently through pass through costs to delivery drivers etc.).

This chart shows the impact of oil prices rising up to $180 per barrel and shows the impact on UK, EU and US inflation rates. All other things being equal, a rise to $180 would add 1.43% to the UK RPI, 1.54% to EU CPI and a massive 4.88% to US CPI. So higher tax rates protect UK and EU consumers against inflation and inflation volatility – not sure they'd see it like that though…

Oil Shocks
Effect on inflation measures of an oil price increase

Oil Price $/Barrel	UK RPI	EA CPI Ex-Tobacco	US CPI
90	0.00	0.00	0.00
100	0.16	0.17	0.54
110	0.32	0.34	1.08
120	0.48	0.51	1.63
130	0.63	0.68	2.17
140	0.79	0.86	2.71
150	0.95	1.03	3.25
160	1.11	0.20	3.80
170	1.27	1.37	4.34
180	1.43	1.54	4.88

High petrol taxes mean that UK + Europe are insulated from crude oil price moves

M&G INVESTMENTS

2   Source: Fathom Consulting as at 28 February 2011

Anyway, elsewhere, I read a review of a BBC2 Horizon programme called Do You See What I See? It looked at sporting results for teams that play in red and blue – there's always been an argument that teams in red do disproportionately well – this looked at a study from the 2004 Olympics, where taekwondo results were analysed. In that sport, red and blue combat gear is assigned at random – yet the results showed that red won 2/3rds of the results. Better still, when the fights were filmed, and the colours reversed digitally, judges watching the recordings still awarded the "red" fighters the bouts. Fascinating stuff – and congratulations Nottingham Forest (in red) on a stunning cup comeback last night versus Notts County!

Chapter 87
Buffett, taxation and the collapse in the average male worker's standard of living

Markus Peters - Wednesday, August 17th, 2011

On Monday Warren Buffett stated "our leaders have asked for 'shared sacrifice'". But when they did the asking, they spared me….whilst most Americans struggle to make ends meet, we mega-rich continue to get our extraordinary tax breaks."

We'd just been looking at the chart below, so the timing of his commentary was good. Whilst mean US male weekly earnings are up 13% in inflation adjusted terms since 1969, this is highly skewed by high earners getting a disproportionate share of the economic gains of capitalism (and government intervention in capitalism!). The median, which measures the middle person in the distribution, has actually fallen by 28% over the same period. At the same time full time employment has fallen by 16.5% for men.

Who's getting richer and who's getting poorer

Change in US male earnings and employment from 1969 to 2009

	MEAN EARNINGS (PERCENT CHANGE)	MEDIAN EARNINGS (PERCENT CHANGE)			EMPLOYMENT (PERCENTAGE POINT CHANGE)		
	Weekly Earnings, Full-Time, Full-Year Workers	Weekly Earnings, Full-Time, Full-Year Workers	Annual Earnings of All Workers	Annual Earnings of Male Population	Working Full-Time	Working Part-Time	Not Working
Ages 25-64	13%	-1%	-14%	-28%	-16.5	4.7	11.8
Ages 30-50	9	-5	-16	-27	-15.5	5.3	10.2
By Education							
Less than High School	-29	-38	-47	-66	-31.8	8.4	23.4
High School Only	-20	-26	-34	-47	-26.2	8.5	17.8
Some College	-13	-17	-24	-33	-19.2	5.6	13.6
College Degree	11	-2	-7	-12	-6.6	0.7	6.0
By Marital Status							
Married	22	-1	-2	-13	-11.6	3.4	8.3
Not Married	12	-2	-14	-32	-11.0	2.1	8.9

NOTE: Adjusted for inflation using the CPI-U. Unless otherwise specified, values refer to men 25-64. "Full-Time, Full-Year Workers" includes men who worked at least 35 hours per week for more than 50 weeks. "Working Full-Time" includes men who worked at least 35 hours per week for at least 40 weeks. "Not working" is defined as having zero earnings in the previous year.

1   Source: Greenstone/Looney 2011, p. 8.

This lack of burden share is also well illustrated by Stephen von Worley's breakdown of the relative U.S. income tax burden over time. Three observations are striking in this context. First, the tax burden was comparatively high in the 1950s and 1960s when the U.S. public debt stayed flat at relatively low levels. Secondly, the Bush administration lowered the tax burden across income levels at a time when the federal debt level had already been at historically high levels. We know how the story has continued. Finally, Buffett and his peers benefitted disproportionately from the Bush administration's fiscal policy.

Interestingly, Jim tore out this newspaper article from the New York Post last time he was in the States. The commentator, Bill O'Reilly is famously right wing, and tries to avoid the real, and obvious conclusions of the survey – whilst it's true that 49% said "no" to the question "do you think our government should redistribute wealth by heavy taxes on the rich?" (a fairly biased question to start with), 47% said "yes, heavy taxes please". It makes the Republican's refusal to even consider tax rises as part of the disastrous debt ceiling negotiations look not just suicidal from a credit rating standpoint, but even undemocratic.

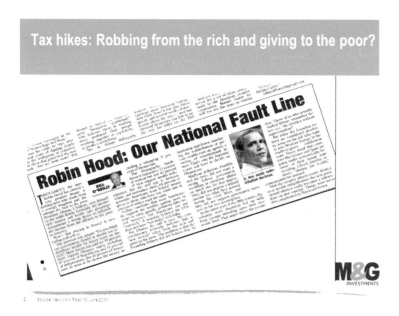

Tax hikes: Robbing from the rich and giving to the poor?

Chapter 88
Ireland (austerity) vs Iceland (default) – who's winning? And a Twitter update…

Jim Leaviss - Friday, September 2nd, 2011

Back in March we wrote about Iceland's response to the banking crisis, and how it differed to other countries that stepped in to support their banking systems. This week, Paul Krugman commented about Iceland's exit from its IMF programme. The IMF has declared that programme successful, and Krugman claims that Iceland is back in the capital markets and has its "society intact". He puts this success down to three things – debt repudiation (default), capital controls and currency depreciation. In fact the opposite of the approach that the distressed Eurozone economies are forced to endure.

Krugman acknowledges that Iceland has a way to go – unemployment is nearer 7% than the 1% it stood at before the crisis. But is default a better option than austerity and an overly hard currency?

Well we have a control of sorts for this experiment. Another member of Alex Salmond's Arc of Prosperity, Ireland is taking the other path. Having borrowed EUR 67.5 billion from the EU and the IMF in 2010, Ireland committed to an aggressive austerity package, and far from defaulting, the government explicitly guaranteed the debts of its broken banking system. The 4 year austerity plan raised sales tax, cut government spending and reduced the minimum wage, with a plan to get the deficit below 3% of GDP by 2014. Is that working?

Well we've just seen quarterly GDP growth of 1.9%, the highest rate since the end of 2007 (most quarters since then have been negative), although unemployment remains around the 14% level, and I guess the best you could say is that it's no longer rising. Stronger exports have helped – domestic weakness persists. One measure that has improved dramatically as a result of the austerity programme has been Ireland's borrowing costs. Since mid July, the longest dated Irish government bond has fallen in yield from 12.5% to under 8.5%, making this one of the best performing bond markets in the world – and in sharp contrast to Spanish and Italian bonds over that period.

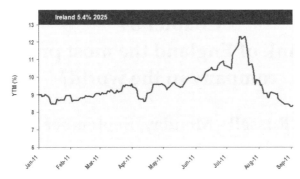

Bond markets like austerity – but only if there's growth too

Source: Bloomberg, as at 2 September 2011

It will be interesting to see which approach to national indebtedness proves most successful over the longer term – I've always said that I thought that an early default against bondholders by the peripheral Europeans was the best outcome for those populations. It's almost certainly what the populations would vote for, if, like the Icelandics, they were offered the choice. Credit rating versus a job for your kids? No contest. As George Osborne follows the austerity path for the UK in defence of its AAA rating (now lost by the US, which then saw one of the biggest ever monthly rallies in its bonds), we're also part of these experiments.

A while ago I wrote about the lack of protest songs http://bit.ly/1iE4Bw from the youth of today. Turns out there were other ways of protesting about being a NEET (not in employment, education or training) than singing, but here's a link to a huge list of 1980s protest songs http://bit.ly/a6nRfT. Also a link to a Billy Bragg article http://bit.ly/rJygpB on a similar theme.

Finally a reminder about our new Twitter feed, @bondvigilantes. We've been going for a couple of weeks now, and as well as linking to this blog, we've tweeted our views throughout the day of the US AAA downgrade, and on our not very widely held assertion that Alistair Darling had a "good" credit crisis.

We also tweeted a link to the new and utterly crucial remastered and complete Smiths box set. Join us, join us.

Chapter 89
Is the Bank of England the most profitable company in the world?

Matthew Russell - Monday, September 5th, 2011

Well the answer is probably no. Exxon Mobil for example made $19 bn last year, and its profits were over $40 bn in 2007. We can also debate whether the Bank of England is a company anyway (it says so on the bank notes, but it was nationalised in 1946).

However, with gilt yields continuing their march downward we thought it would be interesting to put an estimate on the returns the Bank of England has generated in the 2 1/2 years following the start of Quantitative Easing (QE). In my back of an envelope analysis I've calculated that the Bank is currently sitting on a profit in the region of £32 bn. On an initial outlay of £198 bn, this represents a return of about 16% (roughly 40/60 split between capital gain and income). On an initial outlay of £198 bn of freshly printed fivers (costs = paper, ink) the return is even better of course. The highest yield that the Bank bought gilts at was 4.62% on 17 July 2009 (some 4.75% 2030s). That was a price of 101.79, compared with 119.53 today.

Clearly the caveat here is that if the bank actually tried to realise this profit I'm pretty sure that 10yr Gilt yields would be significantly higher than 2.3%, where they stood this morning. With more poor UK data out this morning (PMI Services survey only just above the magic 50 mark), the market's rally today can be at least partly explained by expectations of more QE – there's an MPC meeting on Thursday, but most expect any announcement to come with the publication of the Inflation Report in November (the usual forum for big policy changes). Whether gilt purchases are an efficient means of monetary stimulus or not is something we can save for another blog…

Chapter 90
The Euro-friendly left is gaining momentum in Germany

Markus Peters - Friday, September 16th, 2011

When I listen to my colleagues or read the English papers, the general consensus is that the Germans don't like the Euro and don't want to fund Greece's bail-outs anymore. Whilst you can hardly argue against this overall impression of German public opinion, the feed-through from that to the German political landscape hasn't necessarily reflected that popular view. In Finland and the Netherlands, Eurosceptic sentiment has created opportunities for increased political mandates for populist right-wing parties which emphasise national interests over the European "project". But that hasn't been the German electoral trend.

The German federal state election results since 2010 reveal that German voters have made a considerable move to the left. In the chart below, we combined the vote share of the three main parties on the left of the political centre – Sozialdemokratische Partei Deutschlands (SPD), Die Grünen (Green Party) and Die Linke (The Left) – and added recent poll results for the Berlin election (18 September) and the general election trend. The combined vote share of these parties is in all elections above 50%, and even above 60% in Hamburg, Bremen, Mecklenburg-Vorpommern and Berlin. This signifies a clear shift in political sentiment, as the comparison with the previous election results shows.

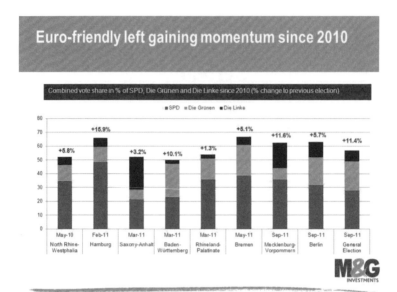

Euro-friendly left gaining momentum since 2010

Combined vote share in % of SPD, Die Grünen and Die Linke since 2010 (% change to previous election)

■ SPD ■ Die Grünen ■ Die Linke

	May-10 North Rhine- Westphalia	Feb-11 Hamburg	Mar-11 Saxony-Anhalt	Mar-11 Baden- Württemberg	Mar-11 Rhineland- Palatinate	May-11 Bremen	Sep-11 Mecklenburg- Vorpommern	Sep-11 Berlin	Sep-11 General Election
	+5.8%	+16.9%	+3.2%	+10.1%	+1.3%	+5.1%	+11.6%	+5.7%	+11.4%

1 Source: www.wahlrecht.de; Berlin and General Election results are based on polls from Emnid as at 4 September 2011.

M&G INVESTMENTS

There are three significant implications of these results. First of all, the centre-right coalition parties have lost the majority in Germany's upper house ("Bundesrat"). That is, this body will have to achieve compromise across party lines until the next major federal state elections which are not due before 2013. As the Bundesrat is meant to vote on legislation regarding European Union affairs, it is not difficult to see that recent complaints about too little involvement in the EFSF reforms will lead to more consultation with the Social Democrats and the Greens. Given the coalition government's recent struggle to find a common position in the Euro crisis, this might not reassure the markets of a strong and clearly unified German position.

Secondly, if voters were aiming at a strengthening of Eurosceptic voices, they will be disappointed in the future. The Social Democrats and the Greens tend to be in favour of European integration and were both strong supporters of the Euro when they were in government. Even The Left, who are less enthusiastic about the Eurozone, don't fundamentally challenge Germany's membership.

Finally, we should keep this recent electoral trend and those two implications in mind when we are debating whether Germany is going to leave the Eurozone or going to chuck anyone else out of the inner circle. I get the feeling that the pro-Euro political powerbase in Germany is often underestimated abroad.

Chapter 91
The new Big Short – EM debt, not so safe

Mike Riddell - Tuesday, September 20th, 2011

A couple of months ago I argued that the implied risk premium on emerging market (EM) debt suggested that the market was treating EM debt as a safe haven, and the market was therefore smoking crack (see this link http://bit.ly/ocgcel). The price action in EM hard currency since then suggests that the EM rally was indeed being artificially stimulated, and 30 year Brazil paper has since sold off almost 100 basis points versus 30 year US Treasuries.

Where it looked like EM still offered value was in FX, i.e. the overheating emerging markets needed to cool down by allowing their currencies to appreciate, while developed countries needed a sharp devaluation to restore competitiveness, restore growth and ultimately reduce debt levels. However while this is what should happen, I now have very little confidence that it actually will happen any time soon.

EM debt has shot the lights out for the best part of a decade as investors have lapped up the strong growth rates, improving debt dynamics, stronger demographics and (particularly of late) much higher yields versus developed markets. These qualities, along with strong historical performance and low historical volatility, have lured a whole wave of investors that previously didn't have any exposure to EM local currency debt, ranging from retail investors to institutional clients, pension funds and sovereign wealth funds. While many of the oft-quoted EM benefits are very valid*, it's important to keep an open mind to the risks facing emerging markets, which very rarely get much coverage (see blog comment on this from last year here).

Right now, the strengthening US Dollar is starting to cause a lot of problems, not so much because external debt is excessive in emerging markets (Eastern

Europe is an exception), but more because one of the most crowded trades in the world is to be long EM FX (specifically Asia FX) and short the US Dollar. Another crowded (albeit slightly stickier) trade is to be long Brazilian Real against the Japanese Yen. Japanese investors have considerable exposure to emerging markets, and JP Morgan has estimated that in the last three years almost ¥6 trillion has flowed from yield-hungry Japanese investors into Brazilian bond or Brazilian Real currency overlay retail investment trusts alone, which equates to about 5% of Brazil GDP. No wonder the Brazilian authorities have struggled to contain BRL appreciation. An unwind of these long EM FX/short USD or JPY trades could cause violent moves.

The most likely cause of a stronger USD or JPY is probably a worsening of the Eurozone debt crisis, which is something we expect as regular readers are probably aware. So if Eurozone weakness and presumably the risk aversion that would accompany it continues to play out, what would the likely effect be on EM local currency debt? Up until last week, EM local currency debt had been remarkably bullet proof in the face of global risk aversion, but this is suddenly starting to change with local currency government bonds and emerging market currencies having sold off sharply in the last week. It looks like the end investors in EM local currency debt are starting to liquidate their holdings, a suspicion strengthened by the Indonesian debt management office yesterday saying that foreign investors' holdings of Indonesian government bonds fell from IDR 251trn on September 9th to IDR237trn on September 16th, a decline of IDR14trn or 5.6% of all foreign owned bonds in just one week. The damage this has done can be seen by Indonesian 10 year government bond yields having soared from 6.5% on September 9th to 7.4% today, while the Indonesian Rupiah has fallen 5.3% against the US Dollar over that time period.

And this is where things start getting scary. The chart below is from an excellent recent note from UBS, where they've taken the average reported foreign held share of local government debt for a sample of major EM countries (Indonesia, Korea, Malaysia, Mexico, Poland and Turkey). Ten years ago EM local currency debt markets were considerably smaller and almost entirely domestic owned, but foreign ownership is now at about 30%. Some may argue that 30% is still not a particularly high figure relative to most developed markets, and that's true, but my main fear is the concentration of holders. For example, the UK government bond market is just under 50% foreign owned, and M&G is one of the larger domestic investors in the gilt market, but we still only own a bit over 1% of it – the gilt market is one of the deepest and most liquid markets in the world. In contrast, there are a handful of enormous global bond investors with a very heavy exposure to local currency emerging market debt, with some owning over 50% of individual EM sovereign bond issues. A reversal of the huge capital inflows into EM debt would result in a total lack of liquidity and significantly higher borrowing costs for emerging market countries. It won't be just the EM sovereigns that have come to rely on these capital flows and the cheap financing this entails; EM banks and to a lesser extent EM corporates are probably in a similar position.

If the recent performance drop in EM debt markets prompts the end investor in EM debt to redeem their holdings then it could rapidly become a systemic event for emerging market economies.

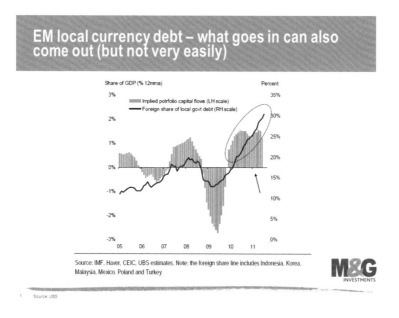

Source: IMF, Haver, CEIC, UBS estimates. Note: the foreign share line includes Indonesia, Korea, Malaysia, Mexico, Poland and Turkey

1   Source: UBS

* The exception being the risk return stats – the experience of the last few years should tell you that things that look great on historical efficient frontiers are bubbles and invariably end up being low return and high risk!

Chapter 92
If this is part 2 of the Great Recession, what were the 10 recent policy errors that got us here?

Jim Leaviss - Friday, September 23rd, 2011

When it was all academic, I enjoyed reading about the causes of the Wall Street Crash, the Great Depression and the German hyper-inflation. Policy errors abounded. The UK going back on to the Gold Standard in the middle of the crisis and sending the economy down into a deflationary spiral. Andrew Mellon, US Treasury Secretary, saying "liquidate labor, liquidate stocks, liquidate farmers, liquidate real estate...it will purge the rottenness out of the system" (and letting the banks go bust). France demanding punitive war reparations from a desperately weak Germany, causing money printing and social unrest.

So if what we're seeing right now is the start of a second wave of the Great Recession, what will historians think were the big policy mistakes in the couple of years since the first down-wave ended in 2009? Here are a few ideas – the 10 recent policy errors that have sent us back to the brink:

1. The **ECB hiking interest rates twice this year** in response to a commodity led inflation overshoot. Whilst I guess this gets reversed next month (or even sooner?) and the ECB cuts, the damage this did to confidence and to European funding costs was significant, not least because it caused the Euro to remain relatively strong. There was no evidence of second round inflationary effects, and the hikes came at a terrible time in the recovery.

2. The Tea Party and **the idiots on both sides of politics in the US** not coming up with even small compromises that would have given S&P an excuse not to downgrade the US from AAA.

3. The continuing Osborne **UK austerity programme**. As economic growth deteriorated, as youth unemployment rocketed and as confidence collapsed, he announced there was no Plan B. "Liquidate, liquidate, liquidate", as Mr Mellon might have said, applauding.

4. **Not banning shorting via sovereign CDS**. We like CDS, we use CDS. But if they didn't exist, the ECB could have aggressively bought peripheral European bonds and driven their yields down. Nowadays, whilst they were doing this in the physical bond market, the market was signalling its disbelief via wider CDS spreads. This visible secondary market doesn't allow anyone to suspend disbelief. The price action in sovereign CDS dominates sentiment – just take a look on Twitter.

5. **Over-regulation of the banking sector**. I'm not sure about this one, because the banks are evil, right? But the backdrop of Dodd-Frank in the US, the global solvency regulations and Basel 3, the ring fencing of retail/investment banking etc. doesn't provide an environment in which bank lending will aggressively recover. That's if you think more bank lending/leverage in the system is a solution to this mess.

6. **Not bailing out Greece/not letting Greece go bust quickly**. It kind of didn't matter which, but one of them could have saved the Eurozone. Greece started to wobble at the end of 2009, so we've had nearly 2 years of sovereign debt uncertainty now. Incidentally, could you compare the clamour for austerity for the Greeks now, to the French demands for implausible payments from Germany after the first world war?

7. **Doing the wrong kind of Quantitative Easing**. Operation Twist? The Fed needed to inject printed money directly into a broken housing market and underwater mortgages, boosting labour mobility and getting cash to those with a high marginal propensity to consume, rather than giving the printed money to investors in assets who didn't do anything with it. QE needed to look a little more fiscal than monetary.

8. **China's pegging of the RMB to the US dollar**, and the consequence of many other countries having a semi peg to the US dollar in order to remain competitive versus China. Currency wars. The RMB is the wrong price – it's artificially too weak and therefore developed countries' currencies are artificially too strong. This led to a race to the bottom to weaken relative to other economies, and that didn't help anyone.

9. There was a brief moment in the quiet year or so that we had, when UK defined benefit pension funds were pretty much fully funded for the first time in years. They could have de-risked and locked in benefits for their members. Now that equity markets are nearly 20% lower, and bond yields have fallen by 1.5% (meaning assets have fallen, and liabilities risen) that's no longer the case.

Pension funds didn't de-risk in the good times, and left millions of workers and pensioners in peril for the future.

10. **Not enough shock and awe**. Policy was always too incremental. The world economy needed huge injections of monetary stimulus and fiscal stimulus. The policy announcements were never enough, and confidence in policy making itself faded away as time went on. Obama would like to extend a tax cut, the Fed will do something to do with the shape of the yield curve, the ECB will buy a few Portuguese bonds, the Bank of England might print £50 billion more. The policy action was too tentative – and there wasn't enough collaboration between policy-makers across the world.

I'm sure you'll disagree, or have other policy errors to add. If so, you can comment below, or tweet me @bondvigilantes.

Chapter 93
10 reasons why EFSF is not the Holy Grail

Mike Riddell - Wednesday, September 28th, 2011

We've had numerous concerns with EFSF ever since it was announced last year. Here's our top 10, in no particular order:

(1) The considerable risk of one or more of the AAA rated guarantors being downgraded, which would threaten EFSF's AAA rating.

(2) The fact that the EFSF's current size and form aren't sufficient to bail out Spain and Italy.

(3) A larger EFSF, which solves point (2), could weigh on sovereign ratings and result in problem (1).

(4) Legal risk. Investors in EFSF bonds have no understanding of what the money is to be used for (initially investors were told the facility was not to be used for bank bailouts but that looks likely to change). And if an EFSF guarantor reneges on its guarantee then there's no payback (so if Slovakia pulls out, Germany just ends up guaranteeing more).

(5) Some of the initial guarantors (Spain and Italy) are themselves in trouble and probably need bailing out. If problem (3) is somehow overcome, then that means more EFSF bonds. But then you run into the problem of fungibility. Each EFSF bond has different guarantors, so the first EFSF bond was issued in January to bail out Ireland. Portugal remains to this day one of the guarantors for that particular bond, despite Portugal itself also needing to be bailed out (the two subsequent EFSF issues were to bail out Portugal, of which obviously neither Portugal nor Ireland are guarantors).

(6) The existence of yet another large AAA rated supranational entity will presumably crowd out private sector issuers, governments and particularly other supranational or agency entities, pushing up borrowing costs. Linked to this, the existence of yet another AAA rated supranational entity will get investors wondering about the strength of the sovereign support for those EU financing structures that (unlike EFSF) don't have an 'explicit' guarantee.

(7) Further down the road, if bank or sovereign restructuring is necessary and the EFSF guarantors need to pay out to the EFSF investors, then the guarantors will need to raise money by issuing bonds, which increases debt levels, which leads you back to point (1).

(8) A sovereign restructuring would be proof that the EFSF support mechanism and fiscal discipline measures have failed. This wouldn't be a surprise – EFSF doesn't reduce debt burdens or encourage debt sustainability. It does nothing to address solvency.

(9) There's been enough trouble designing the EFSF, but it is only supposed to last until 2013, at which point we start all over again with the European Stability Mechanism (ESM). And the ESM potentially subordinates the EFSF, taking seniority over existing creditors.

(10) EFSF is not prefunded. Investors need to be persuaded to part with billions of euros to invest in a vehicle with an ever-expanding mandate that lends money to European governments and banks at precisely the time when the market has decided that those governments and banks are insolvent.

Let's focus on the last point. So far only €13bn of EFSF bonds have been issued; two five year bonds and one ten year bond. It looks like the intention is for many, many billions more to be issued. So the supply of EFSF bonds sharply increases, and at the same time, investor demand will likely fall as investors become increasingly uncomfortable about lending to the EFSF for all the reasons listed above. Supply up, demand down, not a good combination.

The chart below shows that the market is already losing confidence. Despite being 'guaranteed' and priced to perform when issued (and hence massively oversubscribed), the first EFSF bonds that came to the market in January now yield 100 basis points more than German government bonds. Curiously they also now yield more than European Investment Bank (EIB) bonds, where EIB debt only has an implicit guarantee from member states. A continuation of this trend will likely result in the ECB being the only end buyer of EFSF, which is something that the Northern Europeans are desperate to avoid.

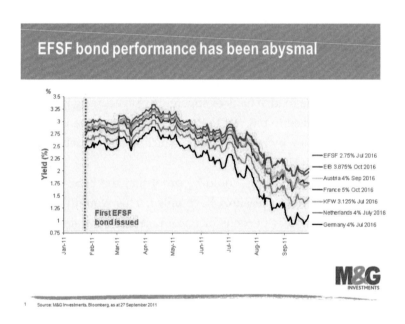

Chapter 94
European High Yield – Crossing the Value Rubicon

James Tomlins - Monday, October 10th, 2011

As we've stated earlier this year, we think the European high yield market is presenting us with some very interesting opportunities. As of 6th October, one of the high yield indices that we track had an average yield to maturity of 12.0%. This equates to a risk premium above and beyond government bonds of around 10.4%, a level that we believe more than compensates investors for expected default risk over the next few years. To put it bluntly, we think high yield bonds are cheap. However, this always begs the (very valid) rejoinder: "Sure it's cheap, but can it get cheaper?"

The age old problem is that investors can be duped by optically cheap valuations only to lose money as the market continues to re-price lower. Timing, at the end of the day, is still a very important consideration. Unfortunately for investors, timing is also one of the hardest things to get right. The best that most humble fund managers can hope for is that the valuation case is so compelling that the potential upside over the medium term can cushion or outweigh any timing errors in the short term.

It was with this in mind that I took a look at the last two market cycles within the European high yield market to investigate the potential medium term impact of any so-called timing errors. The results were intriguing.

What the chart shows below is the credit spread of a Merrill Lynch High Yield Index on the left hand side (the additional yield above government bonds shown in 1,000th's of a %). On the right hand side, the bars up and down show the rolling return over the next 2 years.

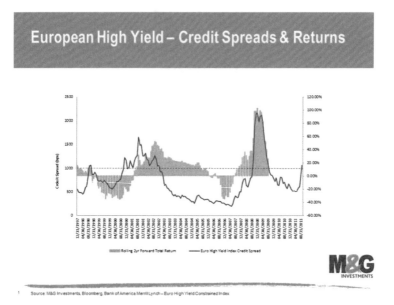

¹ Source: M&G Investments, Bloomberg, Bank of America Merrill Lynch – Euro High Yield Constrained Index

Focusing above the dotted red line, when credit spreads are over 10% (or when valuations suggest the market is cheap) the chart shows us that investing in the high yield market early in the TMT/Dot Com sell off of 2000/2001 would have led to negative returns over the next 2 years. Consequently, the chances of making a timing error were present early in the cycle despite the attractive valuations. The key reason, in my view, was the length and nature of the ensuing default cycle over the following 2 years. This was a fairly brutal default cycle, particularly for the telecommunications and cable sectors. Also, credit spreads remained elevated for quite a long time which denied investors the following wind of falling risk premia. Nevertheless, buying into the high yield market when spreads were over 10% would have generated attractive returns over the following 2 years roughly 75% of the time.

Contrast this to the post-Lehman sell off. Even though spreads peaked at far higher levels than 10%, the scope for making a "timing error" was literally zero using the same criteria. Total returns over the next 2 years were both consistently positive and high when credit spreads were over 10%. The key driver behind this is twofold. Firstly, the default cycle post-Lehman was fairly short and sharp and the sector with the highest default rate was banking & finance (not traditionally a large component of the high yield market). Secondly, the speed and scale of the market recovery meant total returns were particularly high in the following 2 years (rapidly falling credit spreads mean rapidly rising bond prices). Consequently, the lack of an extended default cycle coupled with a rapid recovery in risk premia generated some very high returns.

What does this mean for the European high yield market now we have crossed the Rubicon of 10% credit spreads once more? Are we set for a long drawn-out default cycle, or a short and rapid snap back in spreads that will swamp any timing error? I believe the answer lies in the nature of the next default cycle.

For what it's worth here are my thoughts:

1) The default cycle will weigh most heavily upon sovereign issuers and banks (this is already happening).

2) I do not think we will see a rapid, sharp fall in risk premia to match the 2009 rally. Policy options this time around are more limited and fiscal constraints more acute.

3) There is some scope for a long drawn-out default cycle – but the risks will be concentrated in the European periphery (fiscal retrenchment and de-leveraging creates a hostile environment for highly leveraged companies exposed to these economies).

If I'm right, the next default cycle will present us with some clear cut opportunities and risks. The risk of "timing errors" is arguably highest within the financial sector and the European periphery. These areas could still present great opportunities in due course, but for now I'd argue that investors need to tread with caution. Go in too early and you run the risk of being swamped by a long drawn-out default cycle, despite optically attractive valuations.

On the other hand, the opportunities in European high yield away from these areas are plentiful. I believe the default cycle for the non-financial and non-peripheral issuers will be much more benign. Accordingly, the scope for so called "timing errors" is greatly diminished and this is where investors can cross the European High Yield Rubicon with much greater confidence.

Chapter 95
Mummies' boys – the number 1 variable for predicting Eurozone sovereign stress?!

Mike Riddell - Thursday, October 20th, 2011

I was reminded today of the tongue-in-cheek chart that we put on this blog a year ago showing the close correlation between sovereign 5 year CDS (i.e. the cost of insuring governments against default) and the percentage of men aged 25-34 who still live with their parents within the Eurozone founder member countries (credit to JP Morgan). This was a prompt to do an update, and the out-performance of both Ireland vs Portugal and Spain vs Italy over the last year has helped improve the correlation further.

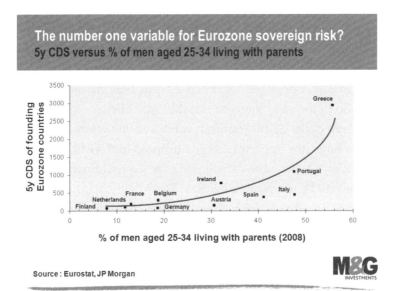

The comment left on last year's blog is of course totally accurate though, i.e. beware mixing up correlation and causation. And for our British readers, the UK fares OK but not wonderfully on this measure, with 20% of men aged 25-34 still living with their folks (see this link http://bit.ly/aIHeua for the full EU list, data as at 2008). I get a feeling this ratio is going to be rising quite a bit over the coming years.

As an aside and looking at what I wrote last year, it's interesting to note that France CDS does now indeed trade wider than Colombia, although Colombia has since been upgraded to investment grade. Next stop for (currently) AAA-rated France is BB rated Philippines. Philippines 5y CDS is currently about 5bps wider than France, and hit a high of 870bps three years ago.

Chapter 96
Pickled Onion Monster Munch – without looking, how many monster feet do you get in a packet?

Stuart Liddle - Friday, October 21st, 2011

Earlier this month the Nobel Prize for Economics went to Sargent and Sims for their work on cause and effect in macro economic policy. All good stuff of course, but it pains us that nobody is looking at the more micro-economic problems of the modern economy – in particular, WHAT KIND OF WORLD IS IT WHERE YOU ONLY GET EIGHT MONSTER MUNCH IN A PACKET?

We have discussed food price inflation in previous blogs and seen how UK supermarkets were able to raise prices and outperform their European peers who had cut prices in periods where commodity prices fell. So when Stefan Isaacs casually commented that Monster Munch appeared to have shrunk in size from when he was a kid, it was time for the kind of quantitative research that modern economists appear so reluctant to perform. Off to the M&G tuck shop we went…

10 monster feet, 10 monster feet, 8 monster feet. Plus some toes. We ran our model and calculated this was an average of 9.33 whole monster feet per packet. It made us wonder – have Monster Munch shrunk? Unfortunately, due to a change in ownership, Monster Munch's holding company couldn't provide me with any statistical information. However due to the popularity of this snack to many an 80's child there is an on-line cult following with numerous people blogging about their experience of the product. So with a little searching it was found that a Monster Munch retailed for around 5-10 pence in 1977 when Monster Munch was launched as "The Biggest Snack Pennies Can Buy", weighing in at 26g. The bag purchased in our canteen a couple of days ago was 45 pence for a smaller bag of 22g.

How does this compare with both food price inflation, and with the price of maize (the biggest ingredient)? Although the price of Monster Munch is soaring above normal food price inflation the price increases are broadly in line with the price of maize. We've plotted two lines though – one just based on the price of a standard size packet of Monster Munch, and one reflecting both that price and the inflation hidden by the shrinkage of the packet. You can see the "hidden" inflation resulting from a 15% reduction in the packet size. This makes an additional large difference to Monster Munch inflation.

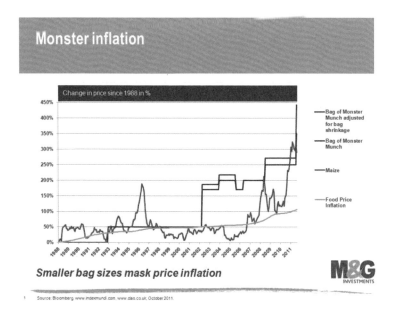

This shrinking of food packaging is something very well known to the Japanese, where despite deflation in the headline numbers for years, the price of instant noodles remained the same – but the size of the plastic tub has been falling year after year. And nearer to home, doing a bit of googling, we found articles referring to a 12.5% fall in the size of Häagen-Dazs ice cream tubs, and a 9% reduction in Scott toilet rolls.

So to address the complaints of our team member, yes you are both getting less snack for your money and it is costing you more.

Chapter 97
What is the increase in US money supply telling us?

Anthony Doyle - Tuesday, October 25th, 2011

Bernanke is clear about why the Fed has embarked on "Operation Twist" – *the Federal Reserve has both greatly increased its holdings of longer-term Treasury securities and broadened its portfolio to include agency debt and agency mortgage-backed securities. Its goal in doing so was to provide additional monetary accommodation by putting downward pressure on longer-term Treasury and agency yields while inducing investors to shift their portfolios toward alternative assets such as corporate bonds and equities.* Bernanke wants investors to take more risk. He would be much happier if there wasn't so much cash sitting on the sidelines. Certainly, negative real cash rates will entice investors to search for higher yielding assets.

Looking at US M2 money supply, an increase of 10.1% over the year to September 2011 should be a cause for concern. A higher rate of money supply growth has occurred on only five occasions since 1984 (including last month). The Fed thinks this is because institutional investors, concerned about exposures of money funds to European financial institutions, shifted from prime money funds to bank deposits, and money fund managers accumulated sizable bank deposits in anticipation of potentially large redemptions by investors. In addition, retail investors evidently placed redemptions from equity and bond mutual funds into bank deposits and retail money market funds.

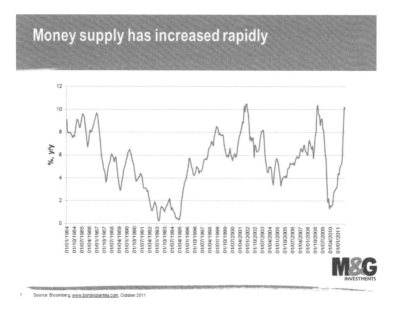

Money supply has increased rapidly

Source: Bloomberg, www.bondvigilantes.com, October 2011

We have always been told that "inflation is always and everywhere a monetary phenomenon". According to economic theory, an excessive expansion of the money supply should be inflationary. Arguably, the current expansion in money supply is not inflationary because banks are not lending. Or are they?

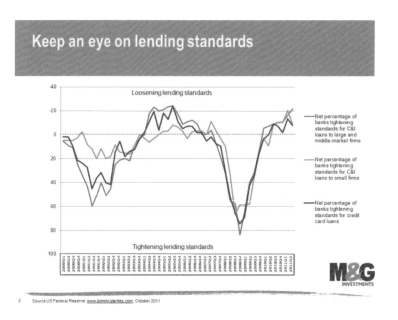

Looking at the Fed's survey on bank lending practices, banks have been loosening lending standards since the third quarter of 2008. The ability of large and medium sized firms to access credit has improved dramatically over the past couple of years. Banks have also reported a loosening in lending standards for credit card loans as well. With the lending standard survey due to be updated at the end of this month, we are keeping a close eye on this indicator. Banks may have reacted to the events of recent months by tightening lending standards again, exactly at a time when the US economy is flirting with recession. On the other hand, ultra-easy monetary policy may result in the banks easing loan standards further in a search for profits.

Some economists believe excess growth in money supply suggests asset price inflation and consumer price inflation. Others believe the increase is a deflationary signal in the short-term as it likely reflects a flight to safety and low expected asset returns. I have some sympathy for this view as the last time year-over-year growth in demand deposits was at current levels the US economy was in a deep recession. The bottom line is, no one knows what impacts extraordinary loose monetary policy is having on the real economy. With so much confusion going on, the only thing that is clear is that central bankers have their work cut out for them in trying to understand this mess. Now we know why economics is the only field in which two people can share a Nobel Prize for saying opposing things.

Chapter 98
Will the Debt Management Office redeem War Loan?

Jim Leaviss - Tuesday, November 1st, 2011

We've written about War Loan before – it's a really interesting gilt, and not only because of its history – it was issued during World War 1 with the 1917 advert stating "if you cannot fight, invest all you can in 5% bonds. Unlike the soldier the investor runs no risk." The "no risk" bit wasn't strictly true. In 1932 its coupon was "voluntarily" reduced from the original 5% to 3 1/2% – I've argued before that this should be viewed a default event for the UK Government (although if UK CDS had existed then, I'm pretty confident ISDA would have considered the debt restructuring 'voluntary'). Additionally, because inflation has at times been way above 3 1/2% in the intervening decades, the real returns have therefore been sharply negative, and as recently as 1990 the bond traded at a price below 30 pence in the £. In the 1970s we're pretty sure the yield of the bond has even been higher than its price – a rare event in bondworld (although Greek bonds have recently seen this happen to them).

As the Eurozone crisis deepens, with last night's decision to hold a referendum in Greece about the bailout causing a big flight to quality in the remaining AAA markets (of which, astonishingly, the UK is one), long dated government bonds are rallying hard. War Loan now trades at a price of 91 1/2. Why this is interesting is that the UK Treasury, via the Debt Management Office (DMO) has the right to call this bond (which has no fixed maturity date – it's a so-called "perpetual" bond) whenever it likes (subject to a notice period) at a price of 100. This has always been academic, as it was so blatantly uneconomical for the taxpayer. But now ultra long gilt yields are hitting record lows. The

Treasury can borrow money until 2060 at a yield of 3.28% at the moment. Theoretically then the authorities can repay holders of War Loan at 100, implying a yield of 3.5%, and reissue new long dated gilts at a yield of 3.28%, saving the taxpayer 22 basis points per year.

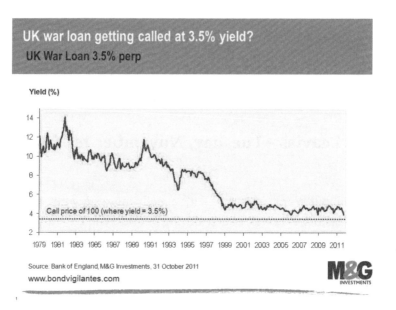

UK war loan getting called at 3.5% yield?
UK War Loan 3.5% perp

Source: Bank of England, M&G Investments, 31 October 2011
www.bondvigilantes.com

So why aren't they doing this? There are perhaps a couple of reasons. Firstly there is a 90 day notice period for such a repayment – the gilt market could move lower again in that period, so making the refinancing look unattractive. Three months is a long time in markets at the moment. So perhaps the market needs to be significantly higher for the DMO to want to do this. Secondly this is not an exact like-for-like switch – it's exchanging a perpetual bond for a dated bond, so at the margin permanent funding for the government is more valuable than dated funding.

This uncertainty makes War Loan difficult to value – and you get paid a premium of 56 basis points (17% more yield) for owning it rather than the fixed date 4% 2060 gilt. It has an uncertain duration – is it a bond with an infinite maturity, or a 90 day maturity? It won't participate in a big rally like a fixed rate bond – would you pay 101 for a bond that might get repaid at par? This is what's known as negative convexity (US mortgage backed bonds also behave like this

– as bond yields fall, more people repay their mortgages to refinance at lower rates, and you find yourself with a shorter duration asset than you might have expected).

Whilst it would be a shame to lose one of the last remaining characterful gilts (since Deputy Governor Paul Tucker was head of the Bank of England's markets division in the mid 1990s there was a deliberate (and necessary) policy to make the gilt market more uniform and transparent, which meant no more perpetual gilts, double-dated gilts and other embedded option gilts), I for one would be happy to see it go. Why? Because – disclaimer – I own it in my gilt fund.

Chapter 99
Why you shouldn't just read the headlines on US unemployment

Anthony Doyle - Thursday, November 3rd, 2011

Everyone is familiar with the deterioration in the US labour market. Figures out today show that the unemployment rate has more than doubled to 9.1% from its pre-crisis low of 4.4% in 2007. The question is how accurately does the unemployment number reflect the true state of the US labour market? To understand this, we need to grasp how the unemployment numbers are compiled.

The Bureau of Labor Statistics (BLS) is responsible for conducting the surveys that inform economists, press, politicians and citizens as to the strength or weakness of the labour market. To do this, the BLS conducts the Current Population Survey (CPS), known as the Household Survey. The CPS has been conducted in the United States every month since 1940.

The BLS calls up around 60,000 households – covering around 110,000 people – every month to find out who is and who isn't working. To get an even spread of responses, the US is split into 2,025 geographic areas. From the 2,025 areas, 824 are selected every month to take part in the survey. The sample is designed to reflect urban and rural areas and different types of employment. Persons are classified as unemployed if they do not have a job, have actively looked for work in the prior four weeks, and are currently available for work.

There are around 115,000,000 households in America, meaning that there is a 0.05% chance that the BLS will call any individual household. Obviously, the majority of households will never be called. If you are lucky enough to be called up, the BLS will ask you a number of questions including:

1. Does anyone in this household have a business or a farm?
2. Last week, did you do any work for (either) pay (or profit)?
3. Last week, did you have a job, either full or part time? Include any job from which you were temporarily absent.
4. Have you been doing anything to find work during the last four weeks?
5. Last week, could you have started a job if one had been offered?

If there is no reason, except temporary illness, that the person could not take a job, he or she is considered to be not only looking but also available for work and is counted as unemployed.

The labour force is made up of the employed and the unemployed. Excluded are persons under 16 years of age, all persons confined to institutions such as nursing homes and prisons, and persons on active duty in the Armed Forces. Everyone else is defined as "not in the labour force". If you are not in the labour force, the BLS will ask you:

1. Do you currently want a job, either full or part time?
2. What is the main reason you were not looking for work during the last four weeks?
3. Did you look for work at any time during the last 12 months?
4. Last week, could you have started a job if one had been offered?

From responses to these questions, the BLS will determine whether or not a person is "marginally attached to the labour force". To be counted as marginally attached to the labour force, individuals must show some degree of labour force attachment by looking and being available for work. "Discouraged workers" are those who are not looking for work because they don't believe there are any jobs, were previously unable to find work, lack the necessary skills or experience to do a job, or face some form of discrimination from employers such as being too young or too old.

If you are "marginally attached to the labour force" or a "discouraged worker", you're out. You are not included in the labour force. When it comes to calculating the unemployment rate, you've disappeared. You are not counted in the official unemployment rate, the rate that everyone uses to understand how well the Fed is doing at achieving its dual mandate of stable prices and full employment. This official unemployment rate, which equals the total number of unemployed as a percent of the labour force, is known to economists as U-3. On this measure, it appears the unemployment rate is now trending lower.

For those who think the U-3 calculation is too stringent (like us) to get the full picture of what is going on in the labour market, the BLS produces a broader measure of unemployment known as "U-6". It basically includes marginally attached and discouraged workers in the unemployment calculation. It also includes those people that are working part-time but would rather be full-time. On this measure, the US labour market appears to be deteriorating once more, and the unemployment rate as calculated by this measure is 16.5%. This suggests around 11.4 million Americans are marginally attached or discouraged workers (from 2001-2008, the number of marginally attached or discouraged workers was on average 5.8m people). According to the BLS, 11.4m Americans do not have an income, do not pay income tax, and do not contribute producing goods and services. Indeed, almost 15% of Americans (45.8m) are now on food stamps. This is a substantial drag on economic growth.

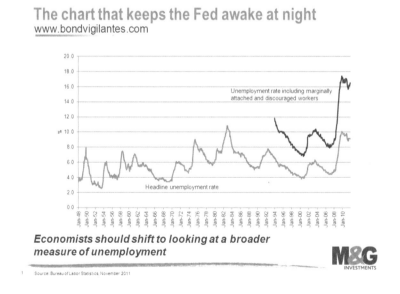

The chart that keeps the Fed awake at night
www.bondvigilantes.com

Unemployment rate including marginally attached and discouraged workers

Headline unemployment rate

Economists should shift to looking at a broader measure of unemployment

M&G INVESTMENTS

1   Source: Bureau of Labor Statistics November 2011

In writing this blog, we've had an eyebrow-raising moment. According to the BLS, the American workforce (employed plus unemployed people) has actually shrunk since October 2008. It doesn't seem to make sense, given most estimates tend to suggest the US population is growing at 1.0% per year, in part due to immigration. We would expect labour force growth to slow due to the retiring cohort of baby boomers and peak in the participation of women in the labour force. But it shouldn't be negative.

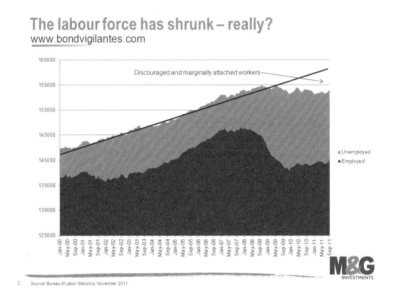

The reason it is negative is because the BLS doesn't count those who are marginally attached or discouraged from entering the labour force (as shown above, around 11.4m people). This has the result of reducing the size of the labour force, resulting in a lower unemployment rate percentage. This is why the official unemployment rate is much lower than the broader U-6 measure and has actually been falling. More and more people are becoming so disenchanted with their job prospects that they have simply stopped looking for a job.

Despite the idiosyncrasies in calculating the unemployment numbers, they are the best we've got. If the Fed is really serious about targeting the unemployment rate – as Chicago Fed President Charles Evans has suggested – then it should have a good hard look at including those people who are underemployed, discouraged or marginally attached to the labour force. The official headline rate – which gets the most coverage amongst the financial community – overstates the current health of the US labour market.

Chapter 100
Did Benford's Law show that Greece fiddled its figures?

Jim Leaviss - Monday, November 7th, 2011

There's a very interesting article in the British Airways in-flight magazine this month by Tim Harford, also known as the Undercover Economist in his FT column. In it, he points out that Benford's Law showed that Greece's reported macroeconomic statistics could have been dodgy well before we knew that for a fact. Benford's Law shows that in real-life data, numbers are distributed in a non-random way. If you look at any collection of numbers – and Harford gives examples of populations of cities, lengths of rivers, or the numbers mentioned in The Economist magazine – the first digit will be 1 in 30% of occasions, with 9 as the first digit only appearing less than 5% of the time.

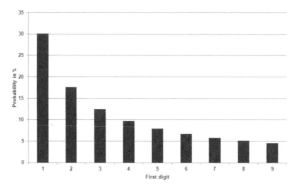

Benford's law states that in lists of numbers, the leading digit is distributed in a specific, non-uniform way

Source: Wikipedia, as at 7 November 2011.

Benford's Law is useful because "real" data exhibits such characteristics, but manipulated data doesn't. Therefore it can be used to analyse data which might be suspected to be fraudulent. And according to the German Economic Review (Fact and Fiction in EU Governmental Economic Data), the Greek economic data was the furthest away from the expected Benford distribution of any EU member state. In particular Greece's data was especially unusual in the year 2000, the year before its entry into the euro…

Acknowledgements

BV book acknowledgements (does not imply they support our views or provide direct research or input to us, just that we have found their work useful and/or interesting!)

Alan James (Barclays)

Alan Clarke (Scotia)

Ralph Segreti (Barclays)

Tim Bond (Odey)

Adam Caplin (BNP Paribas)

John Wraith (Merrill Lynch)

Andrew Roberts (RBS)

Bob Janjuah (Nomura)

Craig Rinder (Lloyds)

Paul Krugman (NYT)

David Parkinson (RBC)

Adam Fergusson (author)

Lucy Shepherd (RBC)

Jackie Ineke (Morgan Stanley)

Cameron Wright (Lloyds)

Tarun Mathur (Barclays)

David Rosenberg (Gluskin Sheff)

Jeff Rosenberg (Blackrock)

Peter Acciavetti (J P Morgan)

Ken Rogoff (academic)

Carmen Reinhart (academic)

Hamish Watson (ex. Bank of England/DMO)

Chris Darkens (Bank of England)

Pieter Fyfer (Credit Suisse)

Michael Lewis (author)

Erik Britton (Fathom Consulting)

Theo Zemek (AXA)

Andrew Ross Sorkin (journalist)

Ranjit Hosangady (UBS)

Andrew Sentance (ex. Bank of England)

Daniel Gabay (Fathom Consulting)

Lawrence Gosling (Incisive Media)

Richard Iley (BNP Paribas)

Steven Hess (Moody's)

Torsten Slok (Deutsche Bank)

David Owen (Jeffries)

Moyeen Islam (Barclays)

Jim Reid (Deutsche Bank)

Thomas Meyer (Deutsche Bank)

Jonathan Brackenbury (Credit Suisse)

Ken Mulkearn (IDS)

Dylan Grice (SocGen)

Albert Edwards (SocGen)

Daniel Lamy (J P Morgan)

Nigel Sargent (Deutsche Bank)

Howard Marks (Oaktree Capital)

Cec Thompson (economist, rugby player)

David Stevenson (journalist)

Index